LITERACY

Ages 6–8

Phon[illegible] dictation

BOOK B

A task-based approach

- Reading practice
- Copying and handwriting
- Comprehension
- Dictation
- Error identification and correction

DIANA RIGG

6334

80/8

Phonic dictation *Book B*

Published by Prim-Ed Publishing® 2012 under licence to PLD Organisation Pty. Ltd.

ISBN 978-1-84654-304-3
PR–6334

Titles available in this series:
Phonic dictation Book A *(Ages 5–7)*
Phonic dictation Book B *(Ages 6–8)*
Phonic dictation Book C *(Ages 7–9)*
Phonic dictation Book D *(Ages 8–10)*

Internet websites

In some cases, websites or specific URLs may be recommended. While these are checked and rechecked at the time of publication, the publisher has no control over any subsequent changes which may be made to webpages. It is *strongly* recommended that the class teacher checks *all* URLs before allowing pupils to access them.

Foreword

Phonic dictation is a series of four books designed to develop pupils' ability to transfer phonic and spelling skills to extended reading and to writing tasks. It focuses on handwriting, letter formation and correct pencil grip and posture. Speech pathologists, occupational therapists and teachers collaborated in the development of this valuable resource.

A short and simple-to-administer placement test can be used to identify at which dictation passage each pupil in your class should start. Pupils complete five tasks for each phonic dictation passage in the book.

Contents

Teachers notes ..... v – vi
Overview of phonic dictation resources for Books A–D vii
Dictation programme placement test viii
Tips for teachers and parents – How to assist pupils when reading and writing ix
The first step to establishing letter formation is having the right posture x
Pencil grip – What is a good pencil grip? xi
– What is NOT a good pencil grip? xii
Position of paper xiii
Am I ready to write? xiv
Curriculum links ..... xv – xvi
Target 1: Dictation tasks that revise phonic concepts: *sh, ch, th, oo, ee, ck, ar, or, ay, ai, er, ing, oy, oi* and *all* 1
sh – Bree's shop 2–3
ch – Chaz and his chum 4–5
th – Theo and his maths 6–7
oo – Mook's book 8–9
oo – A din as the moon comes up 10–11
ee – The leech's speech 12–13
ck – Rick lost his clock 14–15
ar – Mark at the market 16–17
or – The short storm story 18–19
ay – Ray's X-ray 20–21
ai – The snail and the quail 22–23
er – Dinner in winter 24–25
ing – The king's ring 26–27
oy – Troy with his toys 28–29
oi – Boiling a gold coin 30–31
all – Balls In the hall 32–33
Checklist for progressing to Target 2 34
Target 2: Dictation tasks that incorporate consonant clusters and double consonants. 35
scr*, *str* and *spr – The striped tiger 36–37
shr*, *str* and *spr – Shrunk 38–39
ang* and *ong – A bad gang 40–41
old – A clown with a cold 42–43
ff – A gruff bluffing troll 44–45
ll – Under a spell 46–47
ss – My poster is a mess 48–49
Checklist for progressing to Target 3 50

See over for Targets 3 and 4

Contents continued

Target 3: Dictation tasks that primarily involve the application of long vowels: *a–e*, *e–e*, *i–e*, *o–e* and *u–e* 51

a–e – The quake 52–53
a–e – The grapes that I ate 54–55
e–e – Pete and Steve 56–57
i–e – Five over to dine for dinner 58–59
i–e – The bride went for a slide 60–61
o–e – Alone on the throne 62–63
o–e – Rose drove home 64–65
o–e – The note in smoke 66–67
u–e – The month of June 68–69
Checklist for progressing to Target 4 70

Target 4: Dictation passage tasks that primarily involve the application of phonic concepts: *oa*, *ow* (as *oa*), *ir* (as *er*), *ur* (as *er*), *er*, *aw* (as *or*), *or*, *ea* (as *ee*), *ee*, *ou*, *ow* (as *ou*), *ew* (as *oo*), *oo*, *ue* (as *oo*), *y* (as *ee*), *kn*, and *y* (as *igh*) 71

oa – A trip to the beach 72–73
oa – The boasting toad 74–75
ow (m***ow***) – Outside the window 76–77
ow (cr***ow***) – The crow in the snow 78–79
oa and ***ow*** – Snowed in 80–81
ir (th***ir***d) – Gavin is thirteen 82–83
ir (d***ir***ty) – Getting dirty 84–85
ur (b***ur***n) – Sunburn 86–87
ur (s***ur***f) and ***ir*** (th***ir***d) – Dirk's surprise 88–89
er, ***ur*** and ***ir*** – Surfing sunburn 90–91
aw (dr***aw***) – A drawing test 92–93
aw (h***aw***k) – The hawk's meal 94–95
aw and ***or*** – Drawing straws 96–97
ea (t***ea***ch) – My teacher 98–99
ea (fl***ea***) – The flea race 100–101
ea and ***ee*** – A day at the beach 102–103
ou – Storm clouds 104–105
ou – The mouse house 106–107
ow (t***ow***n) – Power off in town 108–109
ow (cl***ow***n) - The brown clown 110–111
ou and ***ow*** – An owl's nest 112–113
ew – Drew's missing screws 114–115
ew and ***oo*** – A tooth in pain 116–117
ue – A rescue helped by a clue 118–119
ue and ***oo*** – Is it true? 120–121
y (pupp***y***) – The puppy with no name 122–123
ee and ***y*** – The puppy and the seeds 124–125
kn – The knight's knife 126–127
y (sp***y***) – The shy spy 128–129

Appendix 131
Template for Task 4: Copying and writing 132–133
Template for Task 5: Dictation 134–135
Templates for Tasks 4 and 5 using different line width and spacing 136–143

Teachers notes

Each phonic dictation passage involves five tasks that support pupil learning:

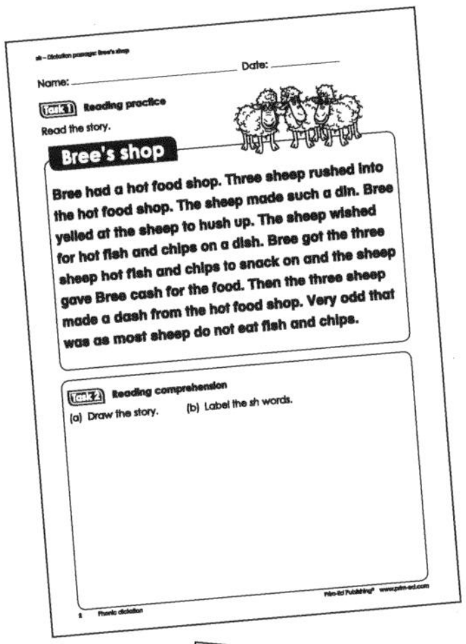

Name: Date:

Task 1 Reading practice

Read the story.

Bree's shop

Bree had a hot food shop. Three sheep rushed into the hot food shop. The sheep made such a din. Bree yelled at the sheep to hush up. The sheep wished for hot fish and chips on a dish. Bree got the three sheep hot fish and chips to snack on and the sheep gave Bree cash for the food. Then the three sheep made a dash from the hot food shop. Very odd that was as most sheep do not eat fish and chips.

Task 2 Reading comprehension

(a) Draw the story. (b) Label the sh words.

Task 1 Reading practice

Pupils read the title and the story.

Task 2 Reading comprehension

Pupils demonstrate their understanding of the passage by illustrating as much as they can of the story, then adding word labels.

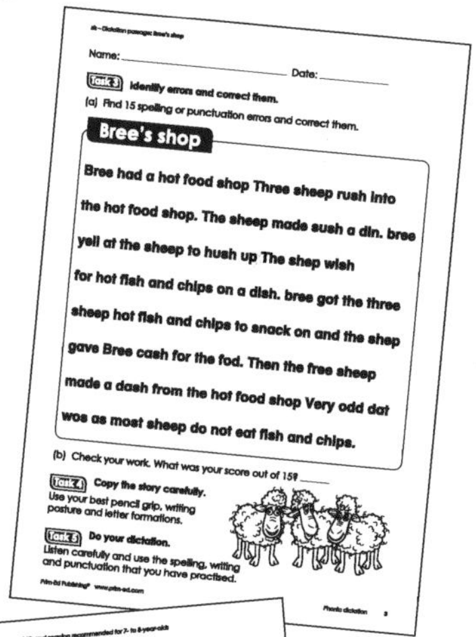

Name: Date:

Task 3 Identify errors and correct them.

(a) Find 15 spelling or punctuation errors and correct them.

Bree's shop

Bree had a hot food shop Three sheep rush into the hot food shop. The sheep made such a din. bree yell at the sheep to hush up The shep wish for hot fish and chips on a dish. bree got the three sheep hot fish and chips to snack on and the shep gave Bree cash for the fod. Then the free sheep made a dash from the hot food shop Very odd dat was as most sheep do not eat fish and chips.

(b) Check your work. What was your score out of 15?

Task 4 Copy the story carefully.

Use your best pencil grip, writing posture and letter formations.

Task 5 Do your dictation.

Listen carefully and use the spelling, writing and punctuation that you have practised.

Task 3 Error identification and correction

There are 15 errors in spelling and punctuation for pupils to identify and correct in the spaces provided on the page.

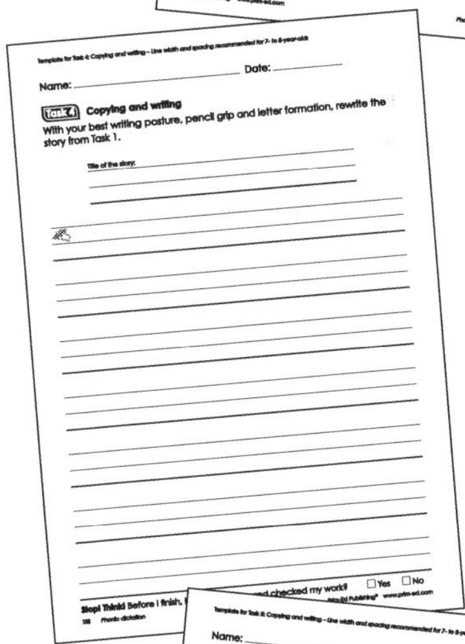

Name: Date:

Task 4 Copying and writing

With your best writing posture, pencil grip and letter formation, rewrite the story from Task 1.

Task 4 Copying and handwriting

Pupils copy the story they have read, focusing on correct posture, pencil grip and letter formation.

There are templates on pages 132 and 133 that can be used for this task.

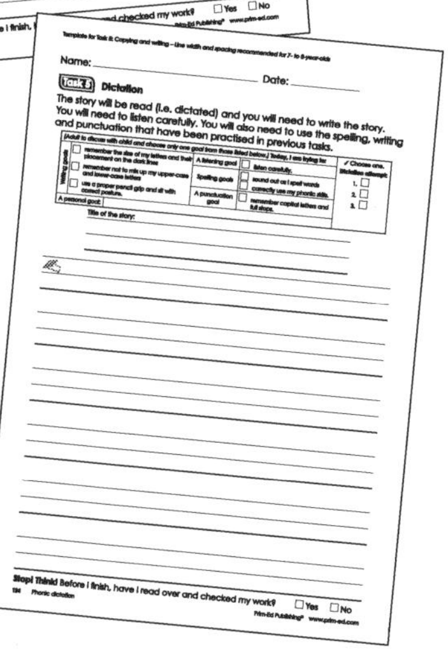

Name: Date:

Task 5 Dictation

Stop! Think! Before I finish, have I read over and checked my work? Yes No

Task 5 Dictation

The story is dictated. Pupils need to listen carefully and remember the spelling, punctuation and writing practised when completing Tasks 1–4. There are templates on pages 134 and 135 that can be used for dictation.

Teachers notes – A note from the author

What happens when correct spelling of test words does not transfer to writing?

Have you noticed how pupils often write words correctly in spelling tests but struggle when applying their new knowledge to written work? Do you wonder why this happens? As a general rule, pupils require many opportunities to rehearse their skills in contexts of increasing complexity. This means if classroom teachers focus on spelling primarily at a single-word level, the transfer to everyday usage will never be guaranteed.

A handy tool for teachers and parents

Dictation tasks require minimal preparation, but hold the potential of producing significant gains in pupil performance. Dictation improves the following skills:

- listening
- auditory memory
- handwriting
- language
- spelling.

Crowd control is essential!

First and foremost, dictation requires pupils' attention. Teachers are required to impose 'crowd control' discipline measures in their classes and remind their pupils what constitutes 'good' listening behaviour.

Dictation tips

1. Before pupils commence a dictation task—i.e. transcribe what they hear—it's recommended they are exposed to the passage beforehand. It's helpful if pupils are able to process its meaning before writing out its parts.
2. When presenting dictation tasks, consider the length of each section verbalised and the number of times the section is repeated before (or while) the pupils transcribe. The shorter the section, the less challenging the dictation task.
3. Repetition of the dictated sections will reduce the memory requirement and make the task less challenging. It is recommended that, over time, the length of each section is gradually extended and the amount of repetition is gradually reduced. This helps pupils apply greater levels of auditory processing and memory.

Dictation aids

The dictation range focuses on a variety of spelling and phonics concepts. As pupils complete the dictation tasks, they are faced with the challenge of applying their recently acquired spelling concepts to the rewriting of passages. This should improve their ability to transfer spelling concepts to their own writing.

Dictation produces significant gains

When presented on a regular basis, dictation tasks hold the potential to produce significant gains in a range of areas. Importantly, dictation assists in the translation of spelling list words to pupils' self-generated writing.

Diana Rigg

BA(Ed), BEd, CPP(UK), MEd, MSc(SpPath)

Overview of phonic dictation resources for Books A–D

Phonic dictation Book A

Contains dictation tasks that primarily involve the application of:

Target 1: Alphabet ***VC*** and ***CVC*** words

Target 2: Phonic concepts—***sh, ch, th, oo, ee, ck***—to ***CVC*** words

Target 3: Blends of ***CCVC*** and ***CVCC*** words

Target 4: Phonic concepts: ***ar***, ***or***, ***ay***, ***ai***, ***oy***, ***oi***, ***er***.

Phonic dictation Book B

Contains dictation tasks that primarily involve the application of:

Target 1: Book A phonic concept revision: ***sh***, ***ch***, ***th***, ***oo***, ***ee***, ***ck***, ***ar***, ***or***, ***ay***, ***ai***, ***er***, ***ing***, ***oy***, ***oi*** and ***all***

Target 2: Consonant clusters and double consonants

Target 3: Long vowels: ***a–e***, ***e–e***, ***i–e***, ***o–e***, ***u–e***

Target 4: Phonic concepts: ***oa***, ***ow*** (m**ow**), ***ir*** (th**ir**d), ***ur*** (b**ur**n), ***er***, ***aw*** (dr**aw**), ***or***, ***ea*** (t**ea**ch), ***ee***, ***ou***, ***ow*** (t**ow**n), ***ew*** (scr**ew**), ***oo***, ***ue*** (bl**ue**), ***y*** (pupp**y**), ***kn***, ***y*** (sp**y**).

Phonic dictation Book C

Contains dictation tasks that primarily involve the application of:

Target 1: A selection of Book A and Book B phonic concept revision: ***bi*** and ***tri consonant clusters***, ***kn***, ***or***, ***aw***, ***ea***, ***ee***, ***y***, ***ly***, ***oo***, ***ue***, ***ew***, ***ai***, ***ay***, ***ow***, ***o-e***, ***oe***, ***oa***, ***ou***, ***er***, ***ir***, ***ur***, and ***squ***

Target 2: Phonemic spelling strategy and phonic concepts: ***igh***, ***y***, ***i-e***, ***tch***, ***ch***, ***ge***, ***dge***, ***ea***, ***ear***, ***eer***, ***ore***, ***oar***, ***oor***, ***our*** and ***silent b***

Target 3: Onset and rime spelling strategy and phonic concepts: ***ace***, ***ice***, ***air***, ***are***, ***ear***, ***eer***, ***ould*** and ***alk***

Target 4: Syllabic spelling strategy and phonic concepts: ***le (ble***, ***dle***, ***fle***, ***gle***, ***kle***, ***ple***, ***tle***, ***zle)***, ***ey***, ***y***, ***be***, ***qu***, ***ph***, ***or***, and ***any***.

Phonic dictation Book D

Contains dictation tasks that primarily involve the application of:

Target 1: A selection of Book C phonic concept revision: ***tch***, ***igh***, ***dge***, ***ge***, ***ey***, ***y***, ***kle***, ***tle***, ***ble***, ***dle***, ***gle***, ***ple***, ***fle***, ***zle***, ***qu***, ***ph***, ***be***, ***silent b*** and ***ea***

Target 2: Spelling involving phonic concepts that change their most regular form: ***a*** (m**a**sk), ***a*** (sw**a**n), ***c*** (**c**ity), ***ch*** (a**ch**e), ***g*** (**g**entle), ***o*** (m**o**nth), ***s*** (**s**ugar), ***or*** (w**or**k), ***u*** (s**u**per and h**u**man), ***u*** (b**u**sy), ***y*** (sh**y** and s**y**mbol)

Target 3: Spelling phonic concepts that incorportate phonemic and/or syllabic spelling strategies: ***age***, ***ture***, ***ear***, ***au***, ***augh*** and ***ough***, ***tion*** and ***sion***, ***ation*** and ***ician***, ***ain***, ***ie***, ***ei***, ***use***, ***our***, ***ous***, ***ine*** and ***sure***

Target 4: Decoding and spelling that involves silent letter phonic concepts: *silent* ***t***, *silent* ***c***, *silent* ***l***, *silent* ***u*** and silent ***w***.

Dictation programme placement test

The following non-standardised spelling test can also be used to establish a general starting point for ***Phonic dictation***.

Task instructions:

Adult says: '*I want you to write a list of words. They start off easy and become more difficult. I will put each of the words into a sentence so you understand what each word is, but I only want you to write the word and not the whole sentence*'.

Book A spelling words

Target	Pattern	No.	Test word	Test sentence
Target 1	CVC	1	**jam**	I had **jam** on my toast.
		2	**wet**	Yesterday, it was **wet** and rainy.
		3	**cup**	Mum drank a **cup** of tea.
Target 2	sh, ch, th	4	**shed**	The lawnmower is kept in the garden **shed**.
		5	**thin**	After his diet, the man became quite **thin**.
		6	**such**	It is **such** a hot day today.
	oo, ee, ck	7	**foot**	I put a shoe on my left **foot**.
		8	**teeth**	The job of a dentist is to check people's **teeth**.
		9	**track**	The racing car sped around the **track**.
Target 3	CCVC	10	**trap**	We caught a mouse in the **trap**.
		11	**drop**	A **drop** of rain landed on my head.
	CVCC	12	**held**	I **held** it tight so that I wouldn't fall.
		13	**sank**	The boat **sank** because it had a hole in it.
Target 4	ay, or, ar, ai	14	**stay**	I am going to **stay** at my friend's house.
		15	**sport**	Tennis is a type of **sport**.
		16	**shark**	The **shark** swam close to the boat.
		17	**paint**	Blue paint was used to **paint** the house.
	er, oi, oy	18	**temper**	The man became very mad and lost his **temper**.
		19	**soil**	The seed was planted in some **soil**.
		20	**boy**	Three girls and a **boy** played in the park.

Scoring/Interpretation: If the pupil spells one or more words incorrectly, within a single target, then he/she requires spelling intervention at that particular stage.

Book B spelling words

No.	Test word	Test sentence
21	**scrap**	He wrote his address on a **scrap** of paper.
22	**spring**	In **spring** the flowers start to bloom.
23	**strict**	The teacher was very **strict**.
24	**shrink**	The magic spell caused the fairy to **shrink** in size.
25	**dress**	The young girl wore a beautiful **dress**.
26	**spell**	The wizard cast a **spell**.
27	**shape**	A circle is a **shape**.
28	**mine**	That toy is not yours. It is **mine**.
29	**smoke**	**Smoke** drifted off the fire.
30	**third**	I came **third** in the race.
31	**window**	A ball broke the glass **window**.
32	**toast**	For breakfast I always eat **toast**.
33	**drew**	The artist **drew** a wonderful picture.
34	**beach**	Many seashells washed up onto the **beach**.
35	**count**	Can you **count** to twelve?
36	**yawn**	People usually **yawn** when they're very tired.

Book C spelling words

No.	Test word	Test sentence
37	**edge**	The **edge** of the cliff is very dangerous.
38	**frighten**	Try not to **frighten** the birds.
39	**kitchen**	Mum prepared dinner in the **kitchen**.
40	**orphan**	John became an **orphan** when his parents died.
41	**instead**	Let's go to the park **instead**.
42	**plumber**	A **plumber** came to fix the leaking pipe.
43	**shuttle**	The **shuttle** bus was 10 minutes late.
44	**chimney**	Smoke rose up through the **chimney**.

Book D spelling words

No.	Test word	Test sentence
45	**ache**	I have an **ache** in my shoulder.
46	**gentle**	The nurse was **gentle** and kind.
47	**symbol**	The ancient **symbol** looked strange.
48	**author**	The famous **author** read his book.
49	**naughty**	My brother can be **naughty**.
50	**excursion**	Our class **excursion** was to the fire station.
51	**pollution**	The factory causes a lot of **pollution**.
52	**harbour**	The fishing boat sailed into the **harbour**.
53	**science**	**Science** is my favourite subject.
54	**wrestle**	My sister likes to **wrestle** with our cousin.

Tips for teachers and parents ...

How to assist pupils when reading

- Most importantly, ensure the pupils have fun and enjoy reading the simple and sometimes silly stories.
- Encourage pupils to go slowly and not rush the reading practice. Always remember to praise pupils' early reading efforts.
- Encourage pupils to 'sound out' (decode) unfamiliar words. Typically, pupils require multiple opportunities to decode before whole-word (or 'sight-word') reading is achieved.
- If pupils are finding the visual element of reading difficult, it is recommended adults use a bookmark to assist pupils to focus on the word or words being read. Another technique that supports the visual aspects of reading is to enlarge the worksheets from an A4 to A3.
- Some pupils require additional reading practice. If this is the case:
  - read the focus story several times on the same day; or
  - read the focus story every day over a week.

  Remember, with **short** and **frequent** practice, reading skills development typically follows.

How to assist pupils when writing

- Most importantly, ensure the pupils have fun and enjoy the rewriting of the simple and sometimes silly stories. Make sure pupils do not rush the writing process. Always remember to praise pupils' early writing efforts.
- Importantly, focus initially on only one goal. Over time, as skills develop, pupils are able to concentrate on multiple goals (e.g. spelling goals, punctuation goals and handwriting goals simultaneously).
- Supporting adults can assist early writing efforts by:
  - sounding out words
  - pointing to a desk strip or chart to prompt the recall of alphabet and/or phonic patterns
  - prompting correct letter formation (e.g. 'Start at the top and go down').
- Some pupils require additional writing practice. If this is the case:
  - read the focus story several times. The more familiar a pupil is with the content of the story, the easier it should be to engage in writing it
  - rewrite the focus story each day over of a week.

  Remember, with **short** and **frequent** practice, writing skill development follows.
- Finally, ask pupils to read their dictated story back to an adult before finishing the task.

The first step to establishing letter formation is having the right posture

A great sitting position at the desk

Keep an eye out:

- for both feet flat on the floor
- for forearms that are resting comfortably on the desk
- that the bottom is placed towards the back of the seat
- that the back is straight and leaning forward slightly, not slumped over the desk or slouched back in the chair.

Front view

Side view

A great standing position

Keep an eye out:

- that weight is evenly distributed over both feet
- that the feet are approximately shoulder width apart
- for a trunk that is fairly straight.

Pencil grip

It is much easier to introduce and reinforce the proper way to hold a pencil than to try to change an inefficient style after the child has used it for several years. Handwriting difficulties can be avoided in later years if there is an early emphasis on developing fine motor skills, learning how to hold a pencil and regular practice.

A proper pencil grip is stable and comfortable, and movements are produced by the smaller muscles of the fingers rather than the whole hand. One important feature of this type of grip is an open and rounded web space (the space formed by the thumb and index finger). It is much harder to move a pencil with finger movements if it is closed.

There are a number of ways to encourage the right grip. For example:

- Make an 'okay' sign with fingers. Place the pencil between the thumb and index fingers, then drop the middle ring and little fingers under the pencil. The last joint of the middle finger sits next to the index finger so it can support the underside of the pencil.
- Children can be reminded to hold their pencil with their 'okay' fingers.
- The pinch action of the index finger and thumb, with the middle, ring and little fingers tucked into the palm, mimics the action of a bird's pecking beak. Children can be reminded to make the bird's beak and hold their pencil.
- Sometimes children find it hard to keep their middle, ring or little fingers tucked into their palm. They often 'climb' onto the pencil shaft. Children can try holding a small marble or wishing stone in the palm of their hand as they write to help them maintain the right grip.
- There are a large number of commercially available pencil grips to help children hold their pencils correctly.
- Extremely short pencils can be used to encourage a child to use fingertips rather than the whole hand.

The shaft of the pencil should rest gently in the webspace. Children can check to see if their pencil is 'lying back on its pillow'.

What is a good pencil grip?

- The pencil shaft is held between the pads of the index finger and the thumb of the dominant hand.
- The middle finger sits along side the index finger, supporting the underside of the pencil.
- The ring and little fingers curl gently into the palm.
- There is an open, fairly circular web space formed by the thumb and index finger. This is where the pencil shaft rests.
- Sometimes the pad of the middle finger is on the pencil, too; this is acceptable if the web space remains open.

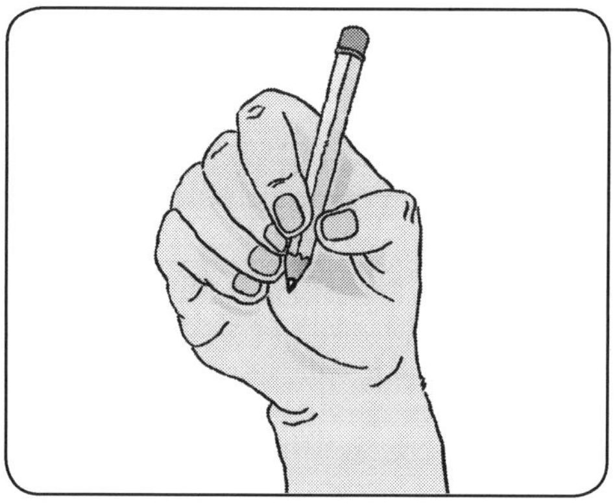

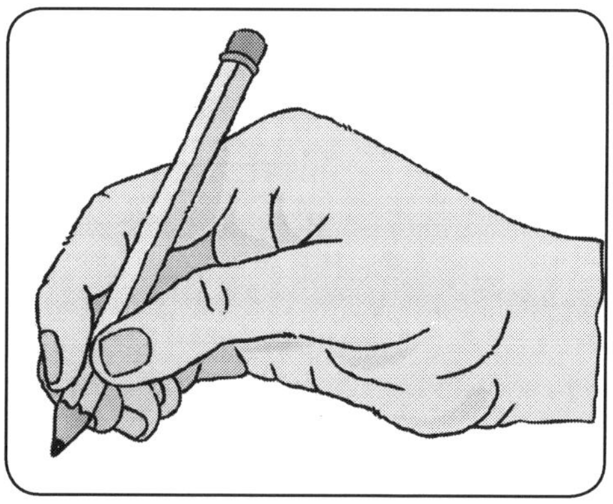

Pencil grip (continued)

What is NOT a good pencil grip?

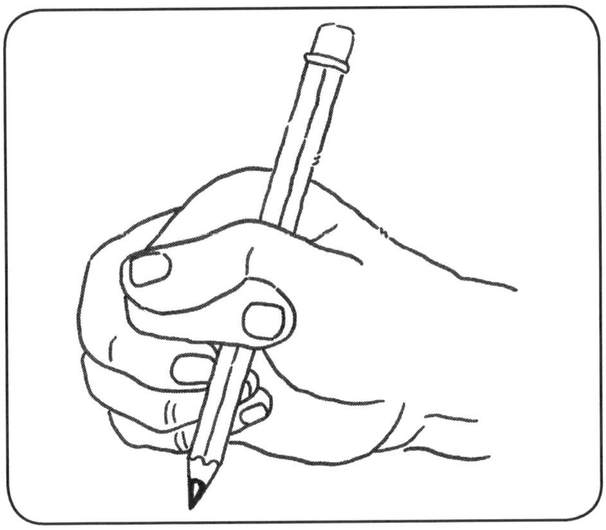

Thumb wrap

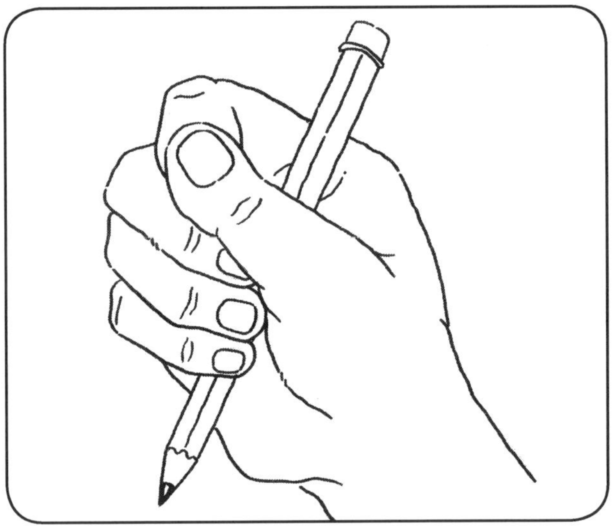

Transpalmar

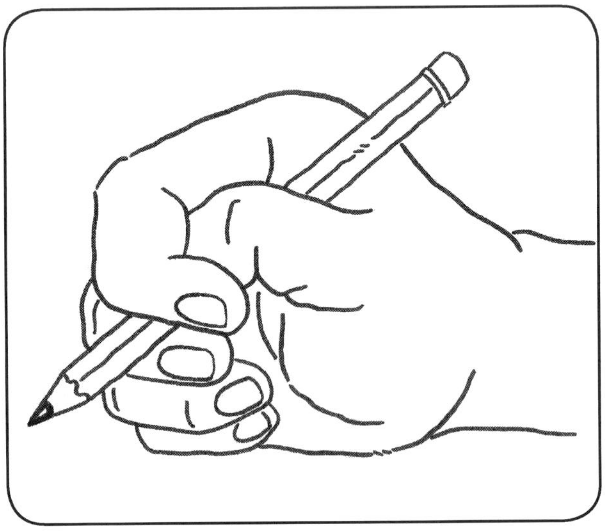

Thumb tuck

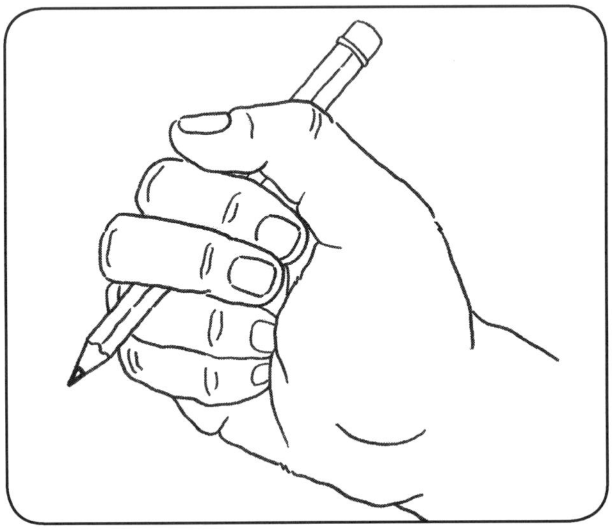

Interdigital brace

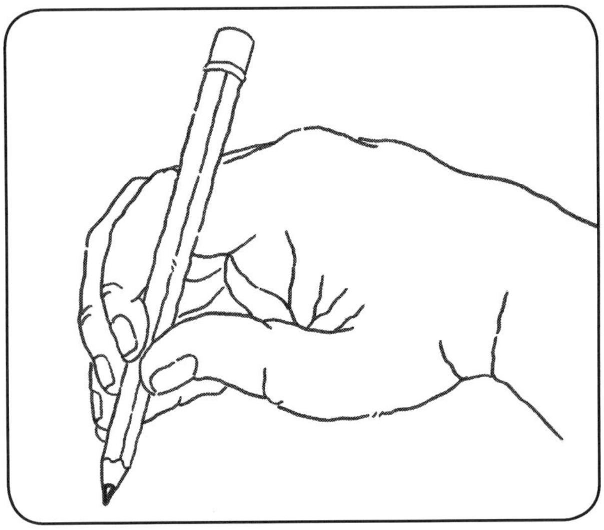

Supinate

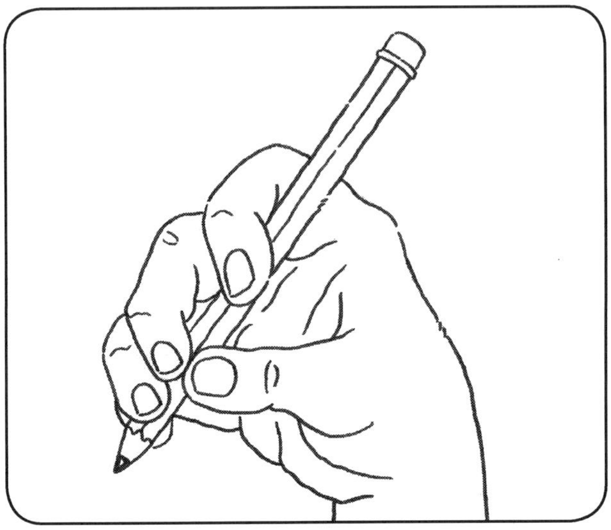

Index grip

Position of paper

Tilt the paper

Before starting to write, it is a good idea to position the paper so that the children can see their work as they go, and can maintain the correct hand position for writing.

Left-handers tilt the top left-hand corner of their page up.

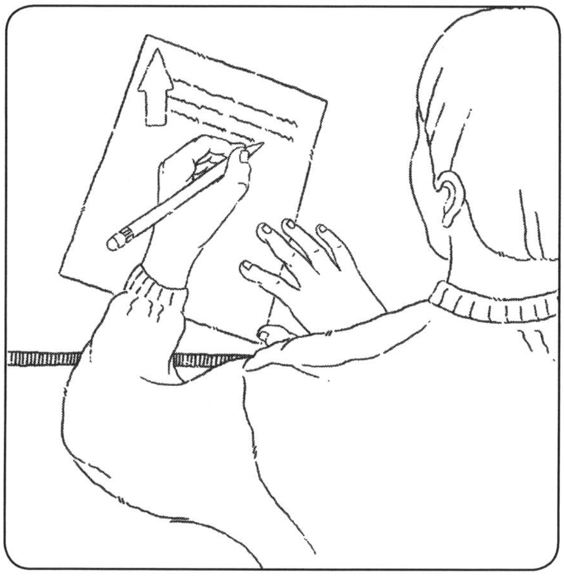

Right-handers tilt the top right-hand corner of their page up.

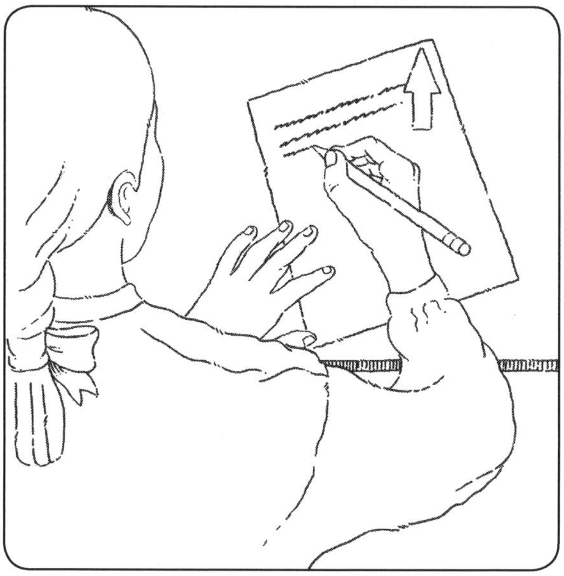

Hold the paper down

Make sure that the non-dominant hand is helping by stabilising the paper.

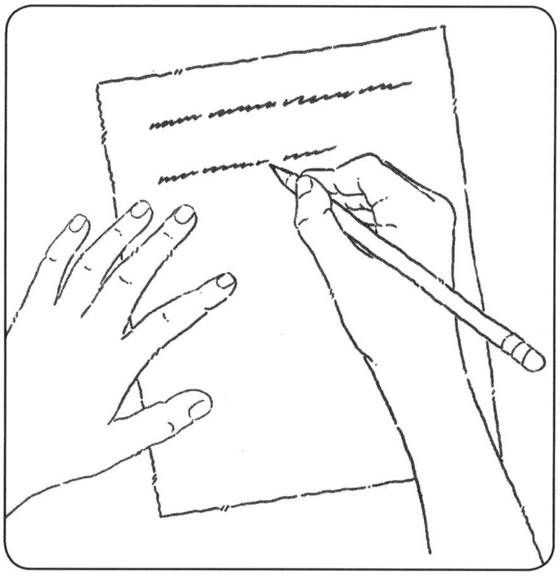

Am I ready to write?

Do I have good posture?

- Sitting back in my chair
- Back straight and leaning slightly forward
- Feet are flat on the floor

Do I have good pencil grip?

The pencil is held between the pads of my index finger and thumb.

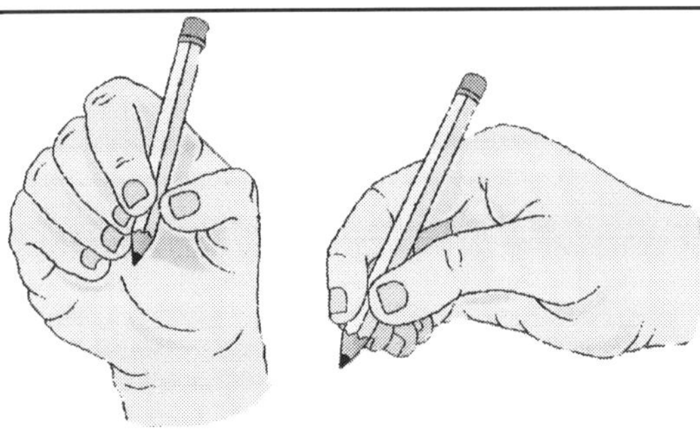

Do I have the paper ready to write on?

The paper is tilted and held steady with my non-writing hand.

Right-handed writers tilt the top right corner of the page up.

Left-handed writers tilt the top left corner of the page up.

Do I have the heel, of my writing hand, on the paper?

This keeps my hand steady so my fingers can do the work.

Now I am ready to write.

Remind pupils of each point before commencing each dictation task.

Curriculum links

England

Subject	Level	Objectives
Literacy	Year 1	**Word recognition: encoding (spelling)** • recognise and use alternative ways of spelling the phonemes already taught; e.g. the /ae/ sound can be spelt 'ai', 'ay' or 'a-e' and know which words contain which spelling alternatives • identify the constituent parts of two-syllable words to support the application of phonic knowledge and skills • recognise automatically an increasing number of familiar high frequency words • apply phonic knowledge and skills when spelling unfamiliar words • spell phonetically decodable two-syllable words **Word structure and spelling** • spell new words using phonics • segment sounds in order to spell them correctly • recognise and use alternative ways of spelling the graphemes already taught; e.g. the /ae/ sound can be spelt 'ai', 'ay' or 'a-e' and know which words contain which spelling alternatives • use knowledge of common inflections in spelling, such as plurals, -ly, -er • spell phonetically decodable two-syllable words **Sentence structure and punctuation** • use capital letters and full stops when punctuating simple sentences
	Year 2	**Word recognition: encoding (spelling)** • spell with increasing accuracy and confidence, drawing on word recognition and knowledge of word structure, and spelling patterns • spell less common alternative graphemes, including trigraphs **Word structure and spelling** • spell with increasing accuracy and confidence, drawing on word recognition and knowledge of word structure, and spelling patterns including common inflections and use of double letters • spell less common alternative graphemes including trigraphs **Sentence structure and punctuation** • use question marks
	Year 3	**Word structure and spelling** • spell high and medium frequency words • spell unfamiliar words using known conventions including grapheme-phoneme correspondences and morphological rules

Curriculum links

Northern Ireland

Subject	Level	Objectives
Language and literacy	Key Stage 1	• use a variety of skills to spell words in their writing • spell correctly a range of familiar, important and regularly occurring words • develop increasing competence in the use of grammar and punctuation
	Key Stage 2	• use a variety of skills to spell words correctly • develop increasing competence in the use of grammar and punctuation

Republic of Ireland

Subject	Level	Objectives
English	1st/2nd Class	• understand the convention of punctuation • spell words in a recognisable way based on awareness of the most common spelling strings and patterns • spell correctly a range of familiar, important and regularly occurring words

Scotland

Subject	Level	Objectives
Literacy and English	First	• spell the most commonly-used words, using knowledge of letter patterns and spelling rules • use appropriate punctuation

Wales

Subject	Level	Objectives
Language, literacy and communication	Foundation	• recognise that punctuation is essential to help a reader understand what is written • develop their ability to spell common and familiar words in a recognisable way
	Key Stage 2	• use punctuation to clarify meaning • use the standard forms of English • develop and use a variety of strategies to enable them to spell correctly

Target 1

Dictation tasks that revise Book A phonic concepts: ***sh, ch***, ***th***, ***oo***, ***ee***, ***ck***, ***ar***, ***or***, ***ay***, ***ai***, ***er***, ***ing***, ***oy***, ***oi*** and ***all***

Target 2

Dictation tasks that incorporate consonant clusters and double consonants

Target 3

Dictation tasks that primarily involve the application of long vowels: ***a–e***, ***e–e***, ***i–e***, ***o–e*** and ***u–e***

Target 4

Dictation tasks that primarily involve the application of phonic concepts: ***oa***, ***ow*** (m***ow***), ***ir*** (th***ir***d), ***ur*** (b***ur***n), ***er***, ***aw*** (dr***aw***), ***or***, ***ea*** (t***ea***ch), ***ee***, ***ou***, ***ow*** (t***ow***n), ***ew*** (scr***ew***), ***oo***, ***ue*** (bl***ue***), ***y*** (pupp***y***), ***kn***, and ***y*** (sp***y***)

Name: ______________________________ Date: ______________

Task 1 **Reading practice**

Read the story.

Bree's shop

Bree had a hot food shop. Three sheep rushed into the hot food shop. The sheep made such a din. Bree yelled at the sheep to hush up. The sheep wished for hot fish and chips on a dish. Bree got the three sheep hot fish and chips to snack on and the sheep gave Bree cash for the food. Then the three sheep made a dash from the hot food shop. Very odd that was as most sheep do not eat fish and chips.

Task 2 **Reading comprehension**

(a) Draw the story. (b) Label the *sh* words.

Name: ______________________ Date: ____________

Task 3 **Identify errors and correct them.**

(a) Find 15 spelling or punctuation errors and correct them.

Bree's shop

Bree had a hot food shop Three sheep rush into the hot food shop. The sheep made sush a din. bree yell at the sheep to hush up The shep wish for hot fish and chips on a dish. bree got the three sheep hot fish and chips to snack on and the shep gave Bree cash for the fod. Then the free sheep made a dash from the hot food shop Very odd dat wos as most sheep do not eat fish and chips.

(b) Check your work. What was your score out of 15? ______

Task 4 **Copy the story carefully.**

Use your best pencil grip, writing posture and letter formations.

Task 5 **Do your dictation.**

Listen carefully and use the spelling, writing and punctuation that you have practised.

Name: ______________________________ Date: ______________

Task 1 **Reading practice**

Read the story.

Chaz and his chum

Chaz was a rich chap from Chad. Rich Chaz had a chat with his chum, Rach. Rich Chaz said to Rach, 'Let's have chips and chops at the beach. It will be such fun'.

So rich Chaz and his chum Rach had lots and lots of chips and chops at the beach. The chums had such a lot of food. The chums had such a lot of fun too.

Task 2 **Reading comprehension**

(a) Draw the story. (b) Label the *ch* words.

Name: ______________________________ Date: ____________

Task 3 **Identify errors and correct them.**

(a) Find 15 spelling or punctuation errors and correct them.

Chaz and his chum

chaz was a rich chap fom Chad Rish Chaz had a chat wiv his chum, Rach. Rich Chaz said to Rach, 'Let's have chips and chops at the beach. It will be such fun'.

so rich Chaz und him chum Rach had lot and lot of chips and chops at the beash. the chums had such a lot of fod The chums had sush a lot of fun too.

(b) Check your work. What was your score out of 15? ______

Task 4 **Copy the story carefully.**

Use your best pencil grip, writing posture and letter formations.

Task 5 **Do your dictation.**

Listen carefully and use the spelling, writing and punctuation that you have practised.

Name: ____________________ Date: ____________

Task 1 **Reading practice**

Read the story.

Theo and his maths

Theo had a maths sum to do. It was a big and hard maths sum. Theo did think and think and think, but Theo did not do the maths sum well. Then Pam went by. Theo said to Pam, 'Can you help me with my maths sum? It is a hard maths sum'.

Then Pam sat and did think of maths. Then Pam did the maths sum. Theo did thank Pam for her help with the maths.

Task 2 **Reading comprehension**

(a) Draw the story. (b) Label the *th* words.

Name: ______________________________ Date: ____________

Task 3 **Identify errors and correct them.**

(a) Find 15 spelling or punctuation errors and correct them.

Theo and his maths

Theo had a maths sum to do. It was a dig and hard maths sam. Theo did think and thik and fink, but Theo did not do the maths sum well. Den Pam wnt by. Theo said to pam, 'Can you hlp me wif my maths sum? it is a hard maths sum'.

then Pam sat and did fink of maths. Then pam did the maths sum. Theo did fank Pam for her hlp with the maths.

(b) Check your work. What was your score out of 15? ______

Task 4 **Copy the story carefully.**

Use your best pencil grip, writing posture and letter formations.

Task 5 **Do your dictation.**

Listen carefully and use the spelling, writing and punctuation that you have practised.

Name: ______________________________ Date: ______________

Task 1 **Reading practice**

Read the story.

Mook's book

Mook was a good cook. Mook the cook was looking in his cookbook when a hook got stuck in his foot. Mook the cook shook his foot this way and that. The hook that was stuck in his foot did fling into Mook's cookbook. 'Look', yelled Mook the cook. 'The hook is stuck in my book.' So Mook the cook took the hook off his cookbook and got back to cooking.

Task 2 **Reading comprehension**

(a) Draw the story. (b) Label the *oo* words.

Name: ______________________________ Date: ____________

Task 3 **Identify errors and correct them.**

(a) Find 15 spelling or punctuation errors and correct them.

Mook's book

Mook was a god cook. Mook the cook was look in his cookbok when a hooc got stuck in his foot. Mook the cook shook his foot dis way and vat. The hook that was stuck in his foot did fing into Mook's cookbok. 'Look', yelled Mook the cook. 'The hook is suck in mi book.' So Mook the cok took the hok off him cookbook and got bak to cook.

(b) Check your work. What was your score out of 15? ______

Task 4 **Copy the story carefully.**

Use your best pencil grip, writing posture and letter formations.

Task 5 **Do your dictation.**

Listen carefully and use the spelling, writing and punctuation that you have practised.

Name: ______________________ Date: ____________

Task 1 **Reading practice**

Read the story.

A din as the moon comes up

Soon the moon will be up and I will need to sleep in my bedroom. But as the moon comes up a din starts. When the moon comes up, bells ring boom-boom and the chicks in the zoo hoot and hoot. As the moon comes up, vans do toot and toot and cows do moo and moo. Such a din gets into my room as the moon comes up.

Task 2 **Reading comprehension**

(a) Draw the story. (b) Label the *oo* words.

Name: ______________________________ Date: ____________

Task 3 **Identify errors and correct them.**

(a) Find 15 spelling or punctuation errors and correct them.

A din as the moon comes up

soon the moon will be up and I will need to seep in my bedroom. But as the mon comes up a din stars. When the mon comes up, bell ring boom-boom and the chiks in the zoo hot and hot. As the moon come up, vans doo toot and toot and cows doo moo and moo. Such a din gets into mi room az the moon come up.

(b) Check your work. What was your score out of 15? ______

Task 4 **Copy the story carefully.**

Use your best pencil grip, writing posture and letter formations.

Task 5 **Do your dictation.**

Listen carefully and use the spelling, writing and punctuation that you have practised.

Name: ______________________________ Date: ____________

Task 1 **Reading practice**

Read the story.

The leech's speech

A leech did a speech. The leech did screech his speech. 'The deep reef is filled with green weed. We all must be keen to meet and go down to the deep reef that is filled with green weed. Indeed we leeches need to seek out who has filled the reef with this green weed.'

The leech that did the speech was glad that all agreed with him. He then let out a big sneeze.

Task 2 **Reading comprehension**

(a) Draw the story. (b) Label the ee words.

Name: ______________________________ Date: ____________

Task 3 **Identify errors and correct them.**

(a) Find 15 spelling or punctuation errors and correct them.

The leech's speech

A leech did a speech. The lech did screech his speesh. 'The deep reef is filled with gween weed. we all must be keen to met and go down to the dep ref that is filled with green wed. Indeed we leeches ned to seek out who has fill the reef with this green weed.'

the leech dat did the speech was gad that all agreed wiv him. He then let out a dig sneeze.

(b) Check your work. What was your score out of 15? ______

Task 4 **Copy the story carefully.**

Use your best pencil grip, writing posture and letter formations.

Task 5 **Do your dictation.**

Listen carefully and use the spelling, writing and punctuation that you have practised.

Name: ____________________ Date: ____________

Task 1 **Reading practice**

Read the story.

Rick lost his clock

Rick the duck lost his clock. Rick the duck looked in his shack, but Rick had no luck. Rick did pick his things up and look, but with no luck. Rick did not find his tick-tock, tick-tock clock. Rick went back into his shack and then to his sack. Rick picked up his sack and tick-tock, tick-tock. In the sack was Rick's clock. Rick the duck has his good luck clock back.

Task 2 **Reading comprehension**

(a) Draw the story. (b) Label the *ck* words.

Name: ______________________________ Date: ____________

Task 3 **Identify errors and correct them.**

(a) Find 15 spelling or punctuation errors and correct them.

Rick lost his clock

rick the duck lost his lock. Rick the duck look in his shack, butt Rick had no luk. Rick did pick his fings up and look, but with no luck Rick did not find his tick-tock, tick-tock clok. Rick wnt back into his chack and then to his sack. rick pick up his sack and tick-tock, tick-tock. In the sock was rick's clock. Rick the duck haz his good luck clock back.

(b) Check your work. What was your score out of 15? ______

Task 4 **Copy the story carefully.**

Use your best pencil grip, writing posture and letter formations.

Task 5 **Do your dictation.**

Listen carefully and use the spelling, writing and punctuation that you have practised.

Name: ______________________ Date: ______________

Task 1 **Reading practice**

Read the story.

Mark at the market

Mark the farmer had been in his garden weeding. Then Mark the farmer went for a rest to lay on his carpet. Then Mark the farmer was alarmed. Mark had left large marks all over his carpet. Then smart Mark sparked up with a plan. He needed to march off to the market to get starch to fix his carpet.

Task 2 **Reading comprehension**

(a) Draw the story. (b) Label the *ar* words.

Name: ______________________________ Date: ____________

Task 3 **Identify errors and correct them.**

(a) Find 15 spelling or punctuation errors and correct them.

Mark at the market

Mark the farmu had been in his garden weedin. Then Mark the farmu went for a rest to la on his carpet. Then Mark the farm was alarm. Mark had left large maks all ovu his carpet. Then sart Mark spark up with a pan. He need to marsh off to the market to get starsh to fiks his carpet.

(b) Check your work. What was your score out of 15? ______

Task 4 **Copy the story carefully.**

Use your best pencil grip, writing posture and letter formations.

Task 5 **Do your dictation.**

Listen carefully and use the spelling, writing and punctuation that you have practised.

Name: ______________________________ Date: ______________

Task 1 **Reading practice**

Read the story.

The short storm story

A stork and a horse ran for forty miles. Forty miles north, the horse and stork got to a corn farm. Then a storm hit the corn farm. The stork and the horse ran up to the farmhouse porch. They were lucky the storm was short. The stork and the horse had a short rest, then the stork and the horse ran the forty miles back. Next time they run for forty miles, they must check for storms.

Task 2 **Reading comprehension**

(a) Draw the story. (b) Label the *or* words.

Name: ____________________ Date: ____________

Task 3 **Identify errors and correct them.**

(a) Find 15 spelling or punctuation errors and correct them.

The short storm story

a stork and a horse ran for forty miles Forty miles norf, the horse and the stork got to a corn frm. Then a stom hit the corn farm The stork and the horse ran up to the farmhouse porch They were lucky the torm was chort. The sork and the horse had a short res, then the stork and the horse ran the fory miles back. Nest time they run for forty miles, they mus chek for storms.

(b) Check your work. What was your score out of 15? ______

Task 4 **Copy the story carefully.**

Use your best pencil grip, writing posture and letter formations.

Task 5 **Do your dictation.**

Listen carefully and use the spelling, writing and punctuation that you have practised.

Name: ____________________ Date: ____________

Task 1 **Reading practice**

Read the story.

Ray's X-ray

Ray had to get an X-ray of his hand. On a day in May, Ray got his X-ray. He did lay on a bed with his hand on a tray. Ray needed his hand to stay still for the X-ray. The X-ray man said to Ray that his X-ray was good, but that today he must rest his hand. By Sunday Ray may play and do things with his hand. Ray did pay for his X-ray, then he went on his way.

Task 2 **Reading comprehension**

(a) Draw the story. (b) Label the *ay* words.

Name: ______________________________ Date: ______________

Task 3 **Identify errors and correct them.**

(a) Find 15 spelling or punctuation errors and correct them.

Ray's X-ray

Ray had to get an X-way of his had. On a day in may, ray got his X-ray. He did lay on a bed with him hand on a tay. Ray need his hand to say still for the X-ray. The X-ray man said to Ray rat his X-ray waz good, but that toda he must rest him hand. by Sunday Ray may play and do thins with his hand. Ray did pay for his X-ra, then he went on his way.

(b) Check your work. What was your score out of 15? ______

Task 4 **Copy the story carefully.**

Use your best pencil grip, writing posture and letter formations.

Task 5 **Do your dictation.**

Listen carefully and use the spelling, writing and punctuation that you have practised.

Name: ______________________ Date: ____________

Task 1 **Reading practice**

Read the story.

The snail and the quail

The snail and the quail had to sail along a brook to a mail train. The snail and the quail had post for the mail train. While the snail and the quail did sail it rained and rained. The snail had a pail to drain the rain from the hull. Then it began to hail. The quail got hit by the hail and was in a bit of pain. Just in time, the snail and the quail got to the mail train with their post. Then the snail and the quail did sail home. This time as they sailed no rain and hail fell.

Task 2 **Reading comprehension**

(a) Draw the story. (b) Label the *ai* words.

Name: ______________________________ Date: ____________

Task 3 **Identify errors and correct them.**

(a) Find 15 spelling or punctuation errors and correct them.

The snail and the quail

The snail and the quail had to sail alon a brook to a mail tail. The sail and the qail had post for the mal tran. While the snail and the quail did sail it rain and rain. The snail had a pail to drain the ran from the hull. Then it began to hal. The quail got hit by the hail and was in a bit of pan. Just in time, the sail and the quail got to the mail train wiv their post. Then the snail and the ail did sail home. This time as they sail no rain and hail fell.

(b) Check your work. What was your score out of 15? ______

Task 4 **Copy the story carefully.**

Use your best pencil grip, writing posture and letter formations.

Task 5 **Do your dictation.**

Listen carefully and use the spelling, writing and punctuation that you have practised.

Name: ______________________ Date: ____________

Task 1 **Reading practice**

Read the story.

Dinner in winter

I have a sister. Her name is Silver. My sister, Silver, sent us a letter. The letter said to come to dinner and the dinner will be in winter by a river. It will be a good dinner even if it will not be in summer. It said we must bring a jumper.

On the day of the dinner in winter it was very wet. My sister, Silver, had a plan and made a hot dinner under a very big tarp. My sister was clever to still have the dinner in a wet winter. The rain never got us as we all sat under the tarp.

Task 2 **Reading comprehension**

(a) Draw the story. (b) Label the *er* words.

Name: ______________________________ Date: ____________

Task 3 **Identify errors and correct them.**

(a) Find 15 spelling or punctuation errors and correct them.

Dinner in winter

I have a sistu. Her name is Silvu. My sister, Silver, sent us a letter The letter said to come to dinner and the dinner will be in witer by a rifer. It will be a good dinner even if it will not be in summer. It said we must bling a jump.

On the da of the dinner in winter it was very wet. My siser, Silver, had a plan and made a hot dinner under a vere big tarp. my sister was clefer to still have the dinner in a wet wint. The rain neber got us as we all sat under the trp.

(b) Check your work. What was your score out of 15? ______

Task 4 **Copy the story carefully.**

Use your best pencil grip, writing posture and letter formations.

Task 5 **Do your dictation.**

Listen carefully and use the spelling, writing and punctuation that you have practised.

Name: ______________________ Date: ____________

Task 1 **Reading practice**

Read the story.

The king's ring

The king bee sat on a swing. The king bee got his kids to sing a song as he sat on his swing. At the end of the song the king bee yelled to his kids to bring him his gold ring. The king's oldest boy had the ring resting on his sting. As he got the king's ring, it fell and did ping as it rolled along. The king was cross that his boy had the gold ring resting on his sting. The king told him off for taking the king's gold ring.

Task 2 **Reading comprehension**

(a) Draw the story. (b) Label the *ing* words.

Name: ______________________________ Date: ______________

Task 3 **Identify errors and correct them.**

(a) Find 15 spelling or punctuation errors and correct them.

The king's ring

The king bee sat on a sing. The king bee got his kids to sing a song as he sat on him swing. at the end of the song the king bee yell to his kids to bing him his god ring. The king's oldest boy had the ring resing on his ting. as he got the king's ring, it fell and did ping as it rolled along. The king was cwoss that his boy had the gold ring resping on him sting. the king told his off for taking the king's gold ping.

(b) Check your work. What was your score out of 15? ______

Task 4 **Copy the story carefully.**

Use your best pencil grip, writing posture and letter formations.

Task 5 **Do your dictation.**

Listen carefully and use the spelling, writing and punctuation that you have practised.

Name: ______________________ Date: ____________

Task 1 **Reading practice**

Read the story.

Troy with his toys

Troy did get spoiled. Troy had many toys. But bad Troy liked to destroy toys. Troy even liked to destroy other boys' toys. One day when Troy was playing with Roy, Troy started to destroy a toy train. Just then Troy's mum did see the toy about to be destroyed. Troy's mum did stop Troy. She yelled, 'If you enjoy playing with the train, do not destroy it'. So then Troy started to play in a good way with the toys.

Task 2 **Reading comprehension**

(a) Draw the story. (b) Label the *oy* words.

Name: ______________________________ Date: ______________

Task 3 **Identify errors and correct them.**

(a) Find 15 spelling or punctuation errors and correct them.

Troy with his toys

Troy did get spoil. Troy had many toys But bad troy liked to destroy toys. Troy even liked to destroy other boys' toys. One day when troy was paying with roy, Troy sarted to destroy a toy train. Just then Troy's mum did see the toy about to be destroyed Troy's mum did stop Troy She yelled, 'If you enjoy play with the train, do not desroy it'. so then roy sarted to play in a good way wir the toys.

(b) Check your work. What was your score out of 15? ______

Task 4 **Copy the story carefully.**

Use your best pencil grip, writing posture and letter formations.

Task 5 **Do your dictation.**

Listen carefully and use the spelling, writing and punctuation that you have practised.

Name: ______________________ Date: ______________

Task 1 **Reading practice**

Read the story.

Boiling a gold coin

Moira joined some silver foil and made it into a coil. Moira then put the silver foil coil with a gold coin resting on it into some oil. As the oil got hot and came to the boil it made a big noise. Then the hot oil started to boil over. Moira had to put soil on the boiling oil to stop it from boiling over. The soil went on the oil and the coin with the foil. I think it was a bad idea to join hot oil, foil and a gold coin together.

Task 2 **Reading comprehension**

(a) Draw the story. (b) Label the *oi* words.

Name: ______________________ Date: ______________

Task 3 **Identify errors and correct them.**

(a) Find 15 spelling or punctuation errors and correct them.

Boiling a gold coin

Moira join some silu foil and made it into a coil. Moira then poot the silvu foil coil with a god coin resting on it into some oil. as the oil got hot and came to the boil it made a dig noise Then the hot oil start to boil over Moira had to put siol on the boil oil to stop it fom boiling over. The soil went on the oil and the coin with the foil. I fink it was a bad idea to join hot oil, foil and a gold coin togeyer.

(b) Check your work. What was your score out of 15? ______

Task 4 **Copy the story carefully.**

Use your best pencil grip, writing posture and letter formations.

Task 5 **Do your dictation.**

Listen carefully and use the spelling, writing and punctuation that you have practised.

Name: ______________________ Date: ______________

Task 1 **Reading practice**

Read the story.

Balls in the hall

All the balls in the hall are kept in a stall. Big balls and small balls are kept in the stall. Red balls and black balls are kept in the stall. As the stall did open, the balls began to fall off the wall and then rolled up a hall. Big balls, small balls, green balls and pink balls did roll up the hall. Such a mess. The balls must go back into the stall.

Task 2 **Reading comprehension**

(a) Draw the story. (b) Label the *all* words.

Name: ______________________________ Date: ____________

Task 3 **Identify errors and correct them.**

(a) Find 15 spelling or punctuation errors and correct them.

Balls in the hall

All the bolls in the hall are kept in a stall big ball and small ball are kept in the stall Red balls and back balls are kept in the stall as the stall did open, the balls began to fall off the wall and ven rolled up a hall Big balls, small balls, geen balls and pik balls did roll up the hall Such a mess. The balls must go bak into the stall.

(b) Check your work. What was your score out of 15? ______

Task 4 **Copy the story carefully.**

Use your best pencil grip, writing posture and letter formations.

Task 5 **Do your dictation.**

Listen carefully and use the spelling, writing and punctuation that you have practised.

Do not progress to Target 2 until ...

☑ Pupils can read the passages that contain *sh, ch, th, oo, ee, ck, ar, or, ay, ai, er, ing, oy, oi* and *all* phonics with minimal errors.

☑ Pupils can complete the dictation tasks with minimal spelling, punctuation and letter formation errors.

Target 1

Dictation tasks that revise Book A phonic concepts: ***sh, ch***, ***th***, ***oo***, ***ee***, ***ck***, ***ar***, ***or***, ***ay***, ***ai***, ***er***, ***ing***, ***oy***, ***oi*** and ***all***

Target 2

Dictation tasks that incorporate consonant clusters and double consonants

Target 3

Dictation tasks that primarily involve the application of long vowels: ***a–e***, ***e–e***, ***i–e***, ***o–e*** and ***u–e***

Target 4

Dictation tasks that primarily involve the application of phonic concepts: ***oa***, ***ow*** (m**ow**), ***ir*** (th**ir**d), ***ur*** (b**ur**n), ***er***, ***aw*** (dr**aw**), ***or***, ***ea*** (t**ea**ch), ***ee***, ***ou***, ***ow*** (t**ow**n), ***ew*** (scr**ew**), ***oo***, ***ue*** (bl**ue**), ***y*** (pupp**y**), ***kn***, and ***y*** (sp**y**)

Name: ______________________________ Date: ______________

Task 1 **Reading practice**

Read the story.

The striped tiger

A striped tiger did sprint into the scrub. Behind the screen of the scrub the striped tiger did wait. The striped tiger did wait for a deer to stroll by. The striped tiger did want the deer to scram. So the strong and swift striped tiger sprang out and the strolling deer sprang off swiftly.

Task 2 **Reading comprehension**

(a) Draw the story. (b) Label the *scr*, *str* and *spr* words.

Name: ______________________________ Date: ______________

Task 3 **Identify errors and correct them.**

(a) Find 15 spelling or punctuation errors and correct them.

The striped tiger

A striped tigu did print into the scrub. Behind the sreen of the rub the riped tiger did wait. The strip tigu did wait for a deer to sroll bi. The stiped tiger did want the deer to scam. So the srong and swif striped tiger prung out and the strolling deer spring off wiftly.

(b) Check your work. What was your score out of 15? ______

Task 4 **Copy the story carefully.**

Use your best pencil grip, writing posture and letter formations.

Task 5 **Do your dictation.**

Listen carefully and use the spelling, writing and punctuation that you have practised.

Name: ______________________________ Date: ______________

Task 1 **Reading practice**

Read the story.

Shrunk

A man shrank to the size of a shrimp. The shrunken man was very stressed. It was not a good thing to be shrunk to the size of a shrimp. The man was not strong. The shrunken man's sprint speed was slow. The shrunken man took a long time to walk down a street. The shrunken man was not thrilled with his size.

Task 2 **Reading comprehension**

(a) Draw the story. (b) Label the *shr*, *str* and *spr* words.

Name: ______________________________ Date: ____________

Task 3 **Identify errors and correct them.**

(a) Find 15 spelling or punctuation errors and correct them.

Shrunk

A man rank to the size of a shrimp. The shruken man was very stress. It wos not a good fling to be shrunk to the size of a rimp. The man was not stong The shrunken man's sprint speed was slow The shrunk man toc a lon time to walk down a reet. The shrunken man was not thilled wiv his size.

(b) Check your work. What was your score out of 15? ______

Task 4 **Copy the story carefully.**

Use your best pencil grip, writing posture and letter formations.

Task 5 **Do your dictation.**

Listen carefully and use the spelling, writing and punctuation that you have practised.

Name: ____________________ Date: ____________

Task 1 **Reading practice**

Read the story.

A bad gang

A gang hung out together. The gang was strong and bad. The bad gang liked to do the wrong things. The bad gang sang bad songs. The bad gang did bang and clang metal poles. The bad gang even liked to spring out and punch those walking by.

Task 2 **Reading comprehension**

(a) Draw the story. (b) Label the *ang* and *ong* words.

Name: ______________________________ Date: ____________

Task 3 **Identify errors and correct them.**

(a) Find 15 spelling or punctuation errors and correct them.

A bad gang

a gang hung out togever. The gang was stong

and bad. The bad gong liked to do the wrong fings

The dad gang sang bad songs The bad gang did

bang and cwang metal poles The bad gang efen

liked to pring out and unch those walk bi.

(b) Check your work. What was your score out of 15? ______

Task 4 **Copy the story carefully.**

Use your best pencil grip, writing posture and letter formations.

Task 5 **Do your dictation.**

Listen carefully and use the spelling, writing and punctuation that you have practised.

Name: ______________________________ Date: ______________

Task 1 **Reading practice**

Read the story.

A clown with a cold

An old bold clown did get a cold. The old clown was not feeling well. The old bold clown did sneeze and sneeze. But the tickets to his show had been sold. So the old bold clown with a cold that had a hold on him, did need to do the show. It was lucky that the show was as good as gold, even if the old bold clown had a bad cold.

Task 2 **Reading comprehension**

(a) Draw the story. (b) Label the *old* words.

Name: ______________________________ Date: ______________

Task 3 **Identify errors and correct them.**

(a) Find 15 spelling or punctuation errors and correct them.

A clown with a cold

an old bold clown did get a cold The old clown was not feel well The old bold clown did sneze and sneze. but the tickets to his show had been sod. So the old bold clown with a cod that had a hold on him, did need to doo the show It was luky that the show was as good as god, efen if the old bold clown had a bad cod.

(b) Check your work. What was your score out of 15? ______

Task 4 **Copy the story carefully.**

Use your best pencil grip, writing posture and letter formations.

Task 5 **Do your dictation.**

Listen carefully and use the spelling, writing and punctuation that you have practised.

Name: ____________________ Date: ____________

Task 1 **Reading practice**

Read the story.

A gruff bluffing troll

A gruff buff old troll did try to call the bluff of three goats. The troll said, 'If you three goats try to cross this bridge, a wind will huff and puff and send you down the cliff'.

Even stiff with fear, the goats did still cross the bridge. No huff or puff of wind came. So the troll did not bluff the three goats.

Task 2 **Reading comprehension**

(a) Draw the story. (b) Label the *ff* words.

Name: ____________________ Date: __________

Task 3 **Identify errors and correct them.**

(a) Find 15 spelling or punctuation errors and correct them.

A gruff bluffing troll

a gruff buff old twoll did try to call the bluff of free

goats The troll said, 'If you thee goats try to coss

this bridge, a wind will huff and puff and send you

down the liff'.

even tiff with fear, the goats did still ross the

bridge No huff or puff of uind came So the toll did

not bluff the ree goats.

(b) Check your work. What was your score out of 15? ______

Task 4 **Copy the story carefully.**

Use your best pencil grip, writing posture and letter formations.

Task 5 **Do your dictation.**

Listen carefully and use the spelling, writing and punctuation that you have practised.

Name: ______________________________ Date: ______________

Task 1 **Reading practice**

Read the story.

Under a spell

A troll did a spell on a gull. The gull did not feel well. The ill gull with a spell on it did then get a chill. The gull stood still but then the poor gull fell. The gull then started to roll. The gull rolled by a mill and by a well. The gull rolled over a doll and over a shell. It was when the troll did yell and ring a bell that the spell did end.

Task 2 **Reading comprehension**

(a) Draw the story. (b) Label the *ll* words.

Name: ______________________________ Date: ____________

Task 3 **Identify errors and correct them.**

(a) Find 15 spelling or punctuation errors and correct them.

Under a spell

A troll did a spell on a gull The goll did not fel well. The ill goll with a spell on it did then get a shill. the gull stood sill but then the poor gull fell. The gull then start to roll. The gull roll by a mill and bi a well. The gull roll over a doll and ovu a shell. It was when the twoll did yill and ring a bell that the pell did end.

(b) Check your work. What was your score out of 15? ______

Task 4 **Copy the story carefully.**

Use your best pencil grip, writing posture and letter formations.

Task 5 **Do your dictation.**

Listen carefully and use the spelling, writing and punctuation that you have practised.

Name: ______________________________ Date: ______________

Task 1 **Reading practice**

Read the story.

My poster is a mess

In art class we made a poster. On my poster I put red gloss paint and green gloss paint. On my poster I put a cross in black and a cross in white. I did press yellow paint onto my poster. I put on a little less pink paint. I did fuss and stress. I did get cross as my poster was a big mess.

Task 2 **Reading comprehension**

(a) Draw the story. (b) Label the *ss* words.

Name: ____________________ Date: __________

Task 3 **Identify errors and correct them.**

(a) Find 15 spelling or punctuation errors and correct them.

My poster is a mess

In art class we made a postu. On my poser I put red gloss pant and green glos pant. On my poster I poot a cwoss in blak and a coss in white. I did press yellow pant onto my poster. I put on a little less pinc pant. I did fus and stress I did get cross as my poster was a big mes.

(b) Check your work. What was your score out of 15? ______

Task 4 **Copy the story carefully.**

Use your best pencil grip, writing posture and letter formations.

Task 5 **Do your dictation.**

Listen carefully and use the spelling, writing and punctuation that you have practised.

Do not progress to Target 3 until ...

- ☑ Pupils can read the passages that incorporate consonant clusters and double consonants with minimal errors.
- ☑ Pupils can complete the dictation tasks with minimal spelling, punctuation and letter formation errors.

Target 1

Dictation tasks that revise Book A phonic concepts: ***sh, ch, th, oo, ee, ck, ar, or, ay, ai, er, ing, oy, oi*** and ***all***

Target 2

Dictation tasks that incorporate consonant clusters and double consonants

Target 3

Dictation tasks that primarily involve the application of long vowels: ***a–e, e–e, i–e, o–e*** and ***u–e***

Target 4

Dictation tasks that primarily involve the application of phonic concepts: ***oa, ow*** (m**ow**), ***ir*** (th**ir**d), ***ur*** (b**ur**n), ***er, aw*** (dr**aw**), ***or, ea*** (t**ea**ch), ***ee, ou, ow*** (t**ow**n), ***ew*** (scr**ew**), ***oo, ue*** (bl**ue**), ***y*** (pupp**y**), ***kn***, and ***y*** (sp**y**)

Name: ______________________ Date: ____________

Task 1 **Reading practice**

Read the story.

The quake

This is a tale of a whale and a snake. The whale and the snake were sleeping in a cave when the walls started to shake. 'It must be a quake', the snake did think. So the snake did run and made it to the gate of the cave. The whale was in a daze. The whale did chase the snake to the gate of the cave and then to the base of the lake where it was safe. The snake was pale and the whale was pale too. At last they were safe.

Task 2 **Reading comprehension**

(a) Draw the story. (b) Label the *a–e* words.

Name: ______________________________ Date: ______________

Task 3 **Identify errors and correct them.**

(a) Find 15 spelling or punctuation errors and correct them.

The quake

This is a tale of a whale and a snake. The whale and the snak were sleping in a cave when the walls start to shake. 'It must be a quake', the snake did fink. So the snake did run and mad it to the gat of the cav. The whale was in a daz. The whale did chase the snak to the gat of the cave and then to the base of the lak where it was safe. the nak was pale and the whal was pale too. At last they were saf.

(b) Check your work. What was your score out of 15? ______

Task 4 **Copy the story carefully.**

Use your best pencil grip, writing posture and letter formations.

Task 5 **Do your dictation.**

Listen carefully and use the spelling, writing and punctuation that you have practised.

Name: ____________________ Date: ____________

Task 1 **Reading practice**

Read the story.

The grapes that I ate

I ate a case of grapes. But the grapes that I ate had a bad taste. The grapes made me feel unwell. The grapes that I ate made me go pale. They made me shake and fall into a daze. But when I became awake, I was brave and I ate more grapes. This time the grapes were safe and tasted fine. I was glad I did not shake and go pale for a second time.

Task 2 **Reading comprehension**

(a) Draw the story. (b) Label the *a–e* words.

Name: ____________________ Date: __________

Task 3 **Identify errors and correct them.**

(a) Find 15 spelling or punctuation errors and correct them.

The grapes that I ate

I at a case of grapes. but the graps that I at had a bad taste. The grapes made me fell unwell. The grapes that I at made me go pale. Thay mad me shake and fall into a daze. but when I became awake, i was brave and I at more grapes. This tim the grapes were saf and tasted fin. I was glad I dod not shake and go pale for a second time.

(b) Check your work. What was your score out of 15? ______

Task 4 **Copy the story carefully.**

Use your best pencil grip, writing posture and letter formations.

Task 5 **Do your dictation.**

Listen carefully and use the spelling, writing and punctuation that you have practised.

Name: ______________________ Date: ____________

Task 1 **Reading practice**

Read the story.

Pete and Steve

Pete and Steve went to the park. Steve yelled to Pete, 'Come here!' Pete ran over to these bushes but he did not find Steve. Again Steve yelled to Pete, 'Come here!' Pete ran to these trees but he did not find Steve. Pete even ran to the bench and the sandpit. Still Pete did not find Steve. Then Pete did find Steve at the swings.

Task 2 **Reading comprehension**

(a) Draw the story. (b) Label the *e–e* words.

Name: ________________________________ Date: ______________

Task 3 **Identify errors and correct them.**

(a) Find 15 spelling or punctuation errors and correct them.

Pete and Steve

Pete and Steve whent to the park. Steve yell to pete, 'Come here!' pete ran ovu to these bushes but he did not find Steve. Again steve yelled to pete, 'Come here!' Pete ran to these tees but he did not find steve. Pete even ran to the bech and the sandpit. Still pete did not finded Steve. Then pete did find steve at the sings.

(b) Check your work. What was your score out of 15? ______

Task 4 **Copy the story carefully.**

Use your best pencil grip, writing posture and letter formations.

Task 5 **Do your dictation.**

Listen carefully and use the spelling, writing and punctuation that you have practised.

Name: ______________________ Date: ____________

Task 1 **Reading practice**

Read the story.

Five over to dine for dinner

A family had invited five over for a meal. The wife decided to spring clean the family home. First she wiped the benches and made them shine. While there, she lined up the forks, knives and spoons. Next she glided into the bathrooms to wipe the shower tiles, before collecting a pile of dirty clothes. The wife raked the garden from side to side before cutting back a vine that had been covering a pine tree. The clean home and garden made the wife smile. It was now a great site for a dinner party.

Task 2 **Reading comprehension**

(a) Draw the story. (b) Label the *i–e* words.

Name: ______________________________ Date: ____________

Task 3 **Identify errors and correct them.**

(a) Find 15 spelling or punctuation errors and correct them.

Five over to dine for dinner

A family had invite five over for a meal. The wife desided to spring clean the famly home. Ferst she wiped the benches and made them shin. While there, she lined up the forks, knifes and spoons. Next she glided into the bathrooms to wip the shower tiles, before collecting a pile of dirte clothes. The wife raked the garen from side to side before cut back a vin that had been covering a pin tree. The clean home and garden made the wif smil. It was now a great site for a dinner parte.

(b) Check your work. What was your score out of 15? ______

Task 4 **Copy the story carefully.**

Use your best pencil grip, writing posture and letter formations.

Task 5 **Do your dictation.**

Listen carefully and use the spelling, writing and punctuation that you have practised.

Name: ______________________ Date: ______________

Task 1 **Reading practice**

Read the story.

The bride went for a slide

The bride did smile as she did stride into her wedding. Bells did chime while songs were sung. The bride had invited nine pals to her wedding. The bride did smile at her nine pals. Just then the bride began to slide and she fell on her side. But the bride picked herself up and then did smile on her way to being a wife.

Task 2 **Reading comprehension**

(a) Draw the story. (b) Label the *i–e* words.

Name: ______________________________ Date: ____________

Task 3 **Identify errors and correct them.**

(a) Find 15 spelling or punctuation errors and correct them.

The bride went for a slide

The bride did smile as she did stride into her weeding. bells did chime while songs were singed. The bride had vited nin pals to her weeding. the brid did smil at her nine pals. just then the bride began to slide and she fell on her sid. but the brid picked herself up and then did smil on her wa to being a wife.

(b) Check your work. What was your score out of 15? ______

Task 4 **Copy the story carefully.**

Use your best pencil grip, writing posture and letter formations.

Task 5 **Do your dictation.**

Listen carefully and use the spelling, writing and punctuation that you have practised.

Name: ______________________ Date: ______________

Task 1 **Reading practice**

Read the story.

Alone on the throne

From time to time the king sat alone on his throne to do his thinking. Speaking to no-one, the king chose his next new laws alone on his throne. Alone on the throne, the king wrote his next speeches in a secret code. The king seated on the throne decided how he would vote in upcoming meetings. The king listed what he hoped for those living in his land. Once all his thinking had been done, the king would leave the throne and return home.

Task 2 **Reading comprehension**

(a) Draw the story. (b) Label the *o–e* words.

Name: ______________________________ Date: ______________

Task 3 **Identify errors and correct them.**

(a) Find 15 spelling or punctuation errors and correct them.

Alone on the throne

From time to time the king sat alon on his thron to do his finking. Speeking to no-one, the king chos his next new laws alon on his thron. Alone on the throne, the king wrot his next speeches in a seret cod. The king seated on the throne decide how he would vote in upcoming meetings. The king listed wot he hoped for those living in his land. Wuns all his finking had been done, the king would leave the throne and turn home.

(b) Check your work. What was your score out of 15? ______

Task 4 **Copy the story carefully.**

Use your best pencil grip, writing posture and letter formations.

Task 5 **Do your dictation.**

Listen carefully and use the spelling, writing and punctuation that you have practised.

Name: ______________________________ Date: ______________

Task 1 **Reading practice**

Read the story.

Rose drove home

Rose drove her car up a slope. Rose even drove her car over a frozen lake. As Rose drove she started to doze. But Rose woke up before she ran off the road. Rose almost did choke when she woke from her doze. It was very lucky that Rose made it to her home. Rose put dinner on her stove then had a good long sleep.

Task 2 **Reading comprehension**

(a) Draw the story. (b) Label the *o–e* words.

Name: ______________________________ Date: ______________

Task 3 **Identify errors and correct them.**

(a) Find 15 spelling or punctuation errors and correct them.

Rose drove home

Rose drov her car up a slope. Rose even drived her car ovu a frozen lake. As rose drived she start to doze. But Rose woke up before she ran off the road. Rose almost did chok when she wok from her doze. it was vere lucke that rose made it to her hom. Rose put dinner on her stov then had a good long seep.

(b) Check your work. What was your score out of 15? ______

Task 4 **Copy the story carefully.**

Use your best pencil grip, writing posture and letter formations.

Task 5 **Do your dictation.**

Listen carefully and use the spelling, writing and punctuation that you have practised.

Name: ______________________ Date: ______________

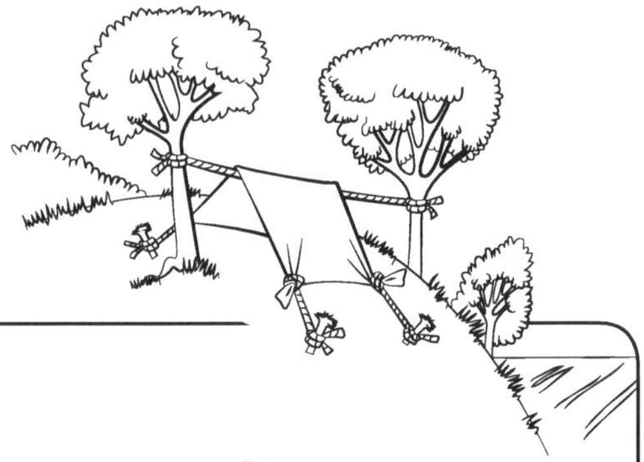

Task 1 **Reading practice**

Read the story.

The note in smoke

Ron camped by a frozen lake. The camp site was on the slope of a hill. Ron took a stove and a tarp with rope to make a tent. Ron camped alone and spoke to no-one. Later Ron did burn wood and the rope. The rope made lots of smoke. Ron sent a smoke code and note home. The note said, 'I will be home soon'.

Task 2 **Reading comprehension**

(a) Draw the story. (b) Label the o–e words.

Name: ______________________________ Date: ______________

Task 3 **Identify errors and correct them.**

(a) Find 15 spelling or punctuation errors and correct them.

The note in smoke

Ron camp bi a frozen lake. The camp site wos on the slope of a hill. ron taked a stove and a tarp with rop to maked a tent. Ron camped alone and spok to no-one. Later ron did burn wood and the rop. The rop made lots of smoke. Ron sent a smok code and note home. The not sed, 'I will be home son'.

(b) Check your work. What was your score out of 15? ______

Task 4 **Copy the story carefully.**

Use your best pencil grip, writing posture and letter formations.

Task 5 **Do your dictation.**

Listen carefully and use the spelling, writing and punctuation that you have practised.

Name: ______________________ Date: ____________

Task 1 **Reading practice**

Read the story.

The month of June

In the month of June I do many things. In June I like to play a tune on my flute. In the month of June I like to make cute red cubes as gifts. In the month of June I like to run down sand dunes. In the month of June I do many things. But in the month of June I am never rude.

Task 2 **Reading comprehension**

(a) Draw the story. (b) Label the *u–e* words.

Name: ______________________ Date: ____________

Task 3 **Identify errors and correct them.**

(a) Find 15 spelling or punctuation errors and correct them.

The month of June

In the month of june I do many fings. In june I like to play a tune on my flute. in the month of june I like to make cute red cubes as gift. in the month of june I like to run don sand dune. In the monf of June I do many thing. but in the month of june I am nevu rude.

(b) Check your work. What was your score out of 15? ______

Task 4 **Copy the story carefully.**

Use your best pencil grip, writing posture and letter formations.

Task 5 **Do your dictation.**

Listen carefully and use the spelling, writing and punctuation that you have practised.

Do not progress to Target 4 until ...

- ☑ Pupils can read the passages that involve the application of long vowels: *a–e, e–e, i–e, o–e* and *u–e* with minimal errors.
- ☑ Pupils can complete the dictation tasks with minimal spelling, punctuation and letter formation errors.

Target 1

Dictation tasks that revise Book A phonic concepts: ***sh, ch***, ***th***, ***oo***, ***ee***, ***ck***, ***ar***, ***or***, ***ay***, ***ai***, ***er***, ***ing***, ***oy***, ***oi*** and ***all***

Target 2

Dictation tasks that incorporate consonant clusters and double consonants

Target 3

Dictation tasks that primarily involve the application of long vowels: ***a–e***, ***e–e***, ***i–e***, ***o–e*** and ***u–e***

Target 4

Dictation tasks that primarily involve the application of phonic concepts: ***oa***, ***ow*** (m***ow***), ***ir*** (th***ir***d), ***ur*** (b***ur***n), ***er***, ***aw*** (dr***aw***), ***or***, ***ea*** (t***ea***ch), ***ee***, ***ou***, ***ow*** (t***ow***n), ***ew*** (scr***ew***), ***oo***, ***ue*** (bl***ue***), ***y*** (pupp***y***), ***kn***, and ***y*** (sp***y***)

Name: ______________________ Date: ____________

Task 1 **Reading practice**

Read the story.

A trip to the beach

A coach drove along a road. In the coach was a groaning goat and a croaking toad. 'How much longer until we reach the coast?' the groaning goat and the croaking toad mumbled.

The road twisted and turned all the way to the coast. Upon reaching the coast, the moaning goat and the croaking toad felt that the beach was too windy and ordered the driver of the coach to take them both home.

Task 2 **Reading comprehension**

(a) Draw the story. (b) Label the *oa* words.

Name: ______________________________ Date: ______________

Task 3 **Identify errors and correct them.**

(a) Find 15 spelling or punctuation errors and correct them.

A trip to the beach

A coach drove along a rod In the coach was a groning goat and a crocking toad. 'Who much longer until we reach the coast' the groaning goat and the croaking toad mumble.

The road twist and turn all the way to the cost. Upon reeching the coast, the moan goat and the crocking toad felt that the beash was too windy and order the driver of the coach to take them both home.

(b) Check your work. What was your score out of 15? ______

Task 4 **Copy the story carefully.**

Use your best pencil grip, writing posture and letter formations.

Task 5 **Do your dictation.**

Listen carefully and use the spelling, writing and punctuation that you have practised.

Name: ______________________ Date: ____________

Task 1 **Reading practice**

Read the story.

The boasting toad

Tom the toad lived on a boat that sailed around a moat. Tom the toad did like to croak and boast about his roasts. He gloated that his roasts were the best in the land. But when the croaking, gloating toad did see that his boasting made the other toads moan and groan, Tom the toad put an end to his boasting ways.

Task 2 **Reading comprehension**

(a) Draw the story. (b) Label the *oa* words.

Name: ______________________________ Date: ____________

Task 3 **Identify errors and correct them.**

(a) Find 15 spelling or punctuation errors and correct them.

The boasting toad

Tom the toad lived on a bot that sail around a moat. Tom the tod did like to crok and boast about his roasts. he goated that his roasts were the best in the land. but went the croaking, gloating toad did see dat his boast made the othu toads moan and gran, tom the tod put an end to his bosting ways.

(b) Check your work. What was your score out of 15? ______

Task 4 **Copy the story carefully.**

Use your best pencil grip, writing posture and letter formations.

Task 5 **Do your dictation.**

Listen carefully and use the spelling, writing and punctuation that you have practised.

Name: ______________________________ Date: ______________

Task 1 **Reading practice**

Read the story.

Outside the window

A small boy rested his elbow on his bedroom windowsill. The small boy looked out his window at everything that was happening. Outside he saw a child throwing a ball and a lazy dog sleeping on a pillow. The small boy saw an old fellow mowing his grass and a boy blowing bubbles. He saw a yellow bird splashing in a shallow pond and yellow flowers growing in a row inside a garden bed. The boy left the window and ran outside.

Task 2 **Reading comprehension**

(a) Draw the story. (b) Label the *ow* words.

Name: ______________________________ Date: ____________

Task 3 **Identify errors and correct them.**

(a) Find 15 spelling or punctuation errors and correct them.

Outside the window

A small boy rest his elbow on his bedroom windowsill. The small boy look out his window at everthing that was happing. Outside he sor a child throwing a ball and a laze dog sleeping on a pillow. The smoll boy saw an old fellow moing his grass and a boy bloing bubble. He saw a yello bird splash in a shallow pond and yellow flowers growing in a row inside a gardn bed. The boy left the windo and ran outsid.

(b) Check your work. What was your score out of 15? ______

Task 4 **Copy the story carefully.**

Use your best pencil grip, writing posture and letter formations.

Task 5 **Do your dictation.**

Listen carefully and use the spelling, writing and punctuation that you have practised.

Name: ______________________ Date: ____________

Task 1 **Reading practice**

Read the story.

The crow in the snow

Nick was a yellow crow. Nick the yellow crow liked the glow of snow. Nick liked to sit on one of the branches of a willow tree and look upon the glowing snow. A boy called Mark also liked snow. Mark liked to rest on his pillow and look out his window at the snow. Every time it snowed the crow came. As soon as the crow came, Mark would sprint out to the snow and throw snowballs at the yellow crow sitting in the willow tree.

Task 2 **Reading comprehension**

(a) Draw the story. (b) Label the *ow* words.

Name: ______________________________ Date: ______________

Task 3 **Identify errors and correct them.**

(a) Find 15 spelling or punctuation errors and correct them.

The crow in the snow

Nick was a yelow crow. Nick the yelow crow liked the glow of sno. Nick liked to sit on one of the branch of a willow tree and look upon the glow snow. A boy called mark also liked snow. Mark liked to rest on his pillo and look out his windo at the sno. Every time it snowed the cro came. As soon as the crow came, Mark would spint out to the sno and thro snowballs at the yello crow sitting in the willo tree.

(b) Check your work. What was your score out of 15? ______

Task 4 **Copy the story carefully.**

Use your best pencil grip, writing posture and letter formations.

Task 5 **Do your dictation.**

Listen carefully and use the spelling, writing and punctuation that you have practised.

Name: ______________________________ Date: ______________

Task 1 **Reading practice**

Read the story.

Snowed in

A toad, a goat and a crow began to moan and groan. They said, 'We need to eat but the snow has floated down and the snow is up to the window. We are snowed in'.

The toad, the goat and the crow did feel like a roast or even a loaf of toast to eat. But the toad, the goat and crow had no roast or toast as the snow was up to the window.

Task 2 **Reading comprehension**

(a) Draw the story. (b) Label the *oa* and the *ow* words.

Name: ______________________________ Date: ______________

Task 3 **Identify errors and correct them.**

(a) Find 15 spelling or punctuation errors and correct them.

Snowed in

A towd, a goat and a croa began to moan and grown. They said, 'We need to eat but the snoa has floated down and the snoa is up to the windoa. We are snowed in'.

The toad, the goat and the croa did feel like a rowst or even a lowf of toast to eat. But the towd, the gowt and crow had no rowst or towst as the snoa was up to the windoa.

(b) Check your work. What was your score out of 15? ______

Task 4 **Copy the story carefully.**

Use your best pencil grip, writing posture and letter formations.

Task 5 **Do your dictation.**

Listen carefully and use the spelling, writing and punctuation that you have practised.

Name: ______________________ Date: ____________

Task 1 **Reading practice**

Read the story.

Gavin is thirteen

Today is May the third. It is Gavin's birthday. Today, Gavin is thirteen years old. Today, Gavin is having a birthday party. It is going to be a rock star birthday party. There are both boys and girls coming to the birthday party. Gavin has thirteen kids invited to his party. First there are games, next there is the cake and the third thing there will be is drinks as all the boys and girls will be thirsty.

Task 2 **Reading comprehension**

(a) Draw the story. (b) Label the *ir* words.

Name: ______________________________ Date: ______________

Task 3 **Identify errors and correct them.**

(a) Find 15 spelling or punctuation errors and correct them.

Gavin is thirteen

Today is may the therd. It is Gavin's berthday. Today, gavin is therteen years old. Today, gavin is having a birthday party. It is going to be a rock sta birthday parte. There are both boys and gerls coming to the birthday party. gavin has thirteen kids invite to his party. Ferst there are games, next there is the cake and the therd thing there will be is drink as all the boys and girls will be thersty.

(b) Check your work. What was your score out of 15? ______

Task 4 **Copy the story carefully.**

Use your best pencil grip, writing posture and letter formations.

Task 5 **Do your dictation.**

Listen carefully and use the spelling, writing and punctuation that you have practised.

Name: ______________________ Date: ____________

Task 1 **Reading practice**

Read the story.

Getting dirty

This morning I started to get dirty when a squirt of paint landed on my shirt. Following this, I became dirtier when I twirled in the playground and thirty specks of mud flew onto my skirt. Later in the day when I began to stir items in a bowl to bake a birthday cake in cooking class, they squirted on my face. Today I was a dirty girl.

Task 2 **Reading comprehension**

(a) Draw the story. (b) Label the *ir* words.

Name: ______________________________ Date: ______________

Task 3 **Identify errors and correct them.**

(a) Find 15 spelling or punctuation errors and correct them.

Getting dirty

This morning I started to get dirty wen a sqirt of paint land on my shirt. Following this, I become dirter when I twirled in the playgrownd and thorty speks of mud floo onto mi skirt. Later in the day wen I began to stir items in a boul to bake a birfday cake in cooking class, they squirt on my face. Today I was a dirte girl.

(b) Check your work. What was your score out of 15? ______

Task 4 **Copy the story carefully.**

Use your best pencil grip, writing posture and letter formations.

Task 5 **Do your dictation.**

Listen carefully and use the spelling, writing and punctuation that you have practised.

Name: ______________________ Date: ____________

Task 1 **Reading practice**

Read the story.

Sunburn

A boy went to church and then he went to surf. He surfed and surfed. He surfed all day long in the boiling hot sun. The surfer got sunburn. The sunburn was so bad that the surfer went to see a nurse. The surfer told her that it really hurt. The nurse gave the surfer some sunburn cream. The nurse told the surfer not to return to the sunshine and not to go surfing until his sunburn had gone.

Task 2 **Reading comprehension**

(a) Draw the story. (b) Label the *ur* words.

Name: ______________________________ Date: ______________

Task 3 **Identify errors and correct them.**

(a) Find 15 spelling or punctuation errors and correct them.

Sunburn

A boy went to cherch and then he wnt to serf. He surf and surf. He surf all day long in the boilin hot sun. The surfur got sunburn. The sunbirn was so bad that the surfu went to see a nurs. The surfer told her that it really hirt. The nurse gave the surfer some sunburn creem. The nirse told the surfer not to retern to the sunshine and not to go surfing until his sunburn had gone.

(b) Check your work. What was your score out of 15? ______

Task 4 **Copy the story carefully.**

Use your best pencil grip, writing posture and letter formations.

Task 5 **Do your dictation.**

Listen carefully and use the spelling, writing and punctuation that you have practised.

Name: ______________________ Date: ____________

Task 1 **Reading practice**

Read the story.

Dirk's surprise

It was Dirk's birthday. Dirk had many surprises. First Dirk was given a shirt. Next Dirk was given a bird. Dirk's third surprise was a surfboard. Dirk surfed and surfed. He swirled, twirled and curled in all the waves. He must have swirled, twirled and curled thirty times in the waves. Dirk did think that the surfboard was the best birthday surprise ever.

Task 2 **Reading comprehension**

(a) Draw the story. (b) Label the *ur* and *ir* words.

Name: ______________________ Date: ____________

Task 3 **Identify errors and correct them.**

(a) Find 15 spelling or punctuation errors and correct them.

Dirk's surprise

It was dirk's birthday. Dirk had many surprises.

Furst Dirk was given a shurt. Next Dirk was given

a berd. Dirk's therd surprise was a sirfboard. Dirk

surf and surf. He swirled, twirled and curl

in all the waves. He must have swerled, twerled and

curled thirte times in the waves. Dirk did fink that

the serfboard was the best burthday surprise ever.

(b) Check your work. What was your score out of 15? ______

Task 4 **Copy the story carefully.**

Use your best pencil grip, writing posture and letter formations.

Task 5 **Do your dictation.**

Listen carefully and use the spelling, writing and punctuation that you have practised.

Name: ______________________ Date: ____________

Task 1 **Reading practice**

Read the story.

Surfing sunburn

Max had been surfing when he got bad sunburn. The sunburn did hurt Max very much. The sunburn even turned into blisters. Max did visit a nurse about his burning and hurting skin. The nurse did burst the sunburn blisters. Next the nurse did squirt cream on the sunburn. Max did need to take a shirt next time he went for a surf.

Task 2 **Reading comprehension**

(a) Draw the story. (b) Label the *er*, *ur* and *ir* words.

Name: ______________________ Date: ____________

Task 3 **Identify errors and correct them.**

(a) Find 15 spelling or punctuation errors and correct them.

Surfing sunburn

Maks had been surf when he got bad sunburn. The sunbern did hurt Max vere much. The sunburn even turn into blister. Max did visit a nurse about his burning and herting skin. The nirse did berst the sunburn blisters. Nekst the nurse did skwirk cream on the sunburn. max did need to take a shurt next time he whent for a sirf.

(b) Check your work. What was your score out of 15? ______

Task 4 **Copy the story carefully.**

Use your best pencil grip, writing posture and letter formations.

Task 5 **Do your dictation.**

Listen carefully and use the spelling, writing and punctuation that you have practised.

Name: ________________________ Date: ____________

Task 1 **Reading practice**

Read the story.

A drawing test

What can you draw? Can you draw a fawn or the paw of a small puppy? Can you draw freshly mowed lawn? Can you draw a tall glass with a straw in it, a baby crawling or an elderly man yawning? Can you draw a prawn in the beak of a hawk or a fawn feeding at dawn? Will you try even though some things on this list are ever so hard to draw?

Task 2 **Reading comprehension**

(a) Draw the story. (b) Label the *aw* words.

Name: ______________________________ Date: ______________

Task 3 **Identify errors and correct them.**

(a) Find 15 spelling or punctuation errors and correct them.

A drawing test

Whot can you draw Can you draw a fawn or the paw of a smoll puppy Can you draw freshle mowed lawn Can you draw a tall glass with a straw in it, a baby crawl or an eldly man yawning Can you dror a prawn in the beek of a hork or a fawn feeding at dawn Will you try even though some thing on this list are ever so hard to draw

(b) Check your work. What was your score out of 15? ______

Task 4 **Copy the story carefully.**

Use your best pencil grip, writing posture and letter formations.

Task 5 **Do your dictation.**

Listen carefully and use the spelling, writing and punctuation that you have practised.

Name: ______________________ Date: ______________

Task 1 **Reading practice**

Read the story.

The hawk's meal

It was dawn when a big hawk saw a prawn. The hawk looked down upon the prawn with open claws. The prawn saw the hawk about to hunt him down and the prawn started to crawl away. It was too late for the prawn. The raw prawn did get trapped in the claws and then the jaws of the hawk. The hawk did yawn after her snack of raw prawn.

Task 2 **Reading comprehension**

(a) Draw the story. (b) Label the *aw* words.

Name: ______________________ Date: ____________

Task 3 **Identify errors and correct them.**

(a) Find 15 spelling or punctuation errors and correct them.

The hawk's meal

It was dorn when a big hork saw a prorn. The hawk look down upon the prawn wiv open clors. the prawn saw the hawk about to hunt his down and the prawn started to crorl away. it was too late for the prawn. the raw prawn did get trapped in the claws and then the jors of the hawk. The hawk did yorn after her snak of ror prawn.

(b) Check your work. What was your score out of 15? ______

Task 4 **Copy the story carefully.**

Use your best pencil grip, writing posture and letter formations.

Task 5 **Do your dictation.**

Listen carefully and use the spelling, writing and punctuation that you have practised.

Name: ______________________________ Date: ______________

Task 1 **Reading practice**

Read the story.

Drawing straws

A horse and a fawn did sit on the lawn. The horse and the fawn did draw straws. The horse held a long straw and a short straw. The fawn got to pick a straw. The fawn did draw a straw. The fawn did draw the short straw. By drawing the short straw the fawn had a job to do. At dawn the fawn had to crawl down to a corn farm. The fawn had to report back with a cob of corn.

Task 2 **Reading comprehension**

(a) Draw the story. (b) Label the *aw* and *or* words.

Name: ____________________ Date: ____________

Task 3 **Identify errors and correct them.**

(a) Find 15 spelling or punctuation errors and correct them.

Drawing straws

A hawse and a fawn did sat on the lorn. The horse and the fawn did dror strors. The horse held a long straw and a short stror. the fawn got to pick a straw. The forn did draw a straw. the fawn did draw the chort straw. by drawing the short straw the fawn had a job to do. At dorn the fawn have to crawl down to a cawn farm. The fawn have to report back with a cob of corn.

(b) Check your work. What was your score out of 15? ______

Task 4 **Copy the story carefully.**

Use your best pencil grip, writing posture and letter formations.

Task 5 **Do your dictation.**

Listen carefully and use the spelling, writing and punctuation that you have practised.

Name: ______________________ Date: ____________

Task 1 **Reading practice**

Read the story.

My teacher

My teacher teaches each of us not to be mean and to join together and work hard as a team. My teacher teaches each of us to read and to finish all work neatly. My teacher teaches each of us to sit up tall and not to daydream. My teacher teaches each of us to eat good foods such as beans, peaches and peas and to eat less ice-cream. My teacher tells each of us to dream big and to reach for all we can be.

Task 2 **Reading comprehension**

(a) Draw the story. (b) Label the *ea* words.

Name: ____________________ Date: __________

Task 3 **Identify errors and correct them.**

(a) Find 15 spelling or punctuation errors and correct them.

My teacher

My teacher teaches eech of us not to be mean and to join togefer and work hard as a teem. My teacher teach each of us to read and to finsh all work neatle. Mi teacher teach each of us to sit up tall and not to daydreem. Mi teacher teaches each of us to eat good foods such as beans, peeches and peas and to eat less ise-cream. My teach tells each of us to dream big and to reash for oll we can be.

(b) Check your work. What was your score out of 15? ______

Task 4 **Copy the story carefully.**

Use your best pencil grip, writing posture and letter formations.

Task 5 **Do your dictation.**

Listen carefully and use the spelling, writing and punctuation that you have practised.

Name: ______________________ Date: ______________

Task 1 **Reading practice**

Read the story.

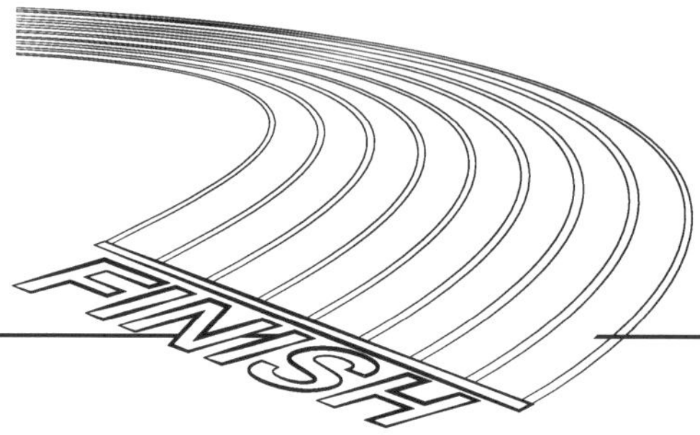

The flea race

Jean was a flea. Jean the flea was entered in a flea race. Jean the flea did reach the finishing line. Jean the flea reached the finish second. Jean got herself a treat as she did reach the finish second. Jean got herself a meal of beans, meat and peach ice-cream. It was a real treat to eat that feast. Jean did think that such a meal was a dream.

Task 2 **Reading comprehension**

(a) Draw the story. (b) Label the *ea* words.

Name: ______________________________ Date: ______________

Task 3 **Identify errors and correct them.**

(a) Find 15 spelling or punctuation errors and correct them.

The flea race

Jean was a flea. jean the flee was enter in a flee race. Jean the flea did reech the finishing line. Jean the flea reached the finsh second. Jean got herself a tweat as she did reach the finish secnd. Jean got herself a meel of beans, meet and peech ice-creem. It was a real treat to eet that feast. Jean did thik that such a meal was a dreem.

(b) Check your work. What was your score out of 15? ______

Task 4 **Copy the story carefully.**

Use your best pencil grip, writing posture and letter formations.

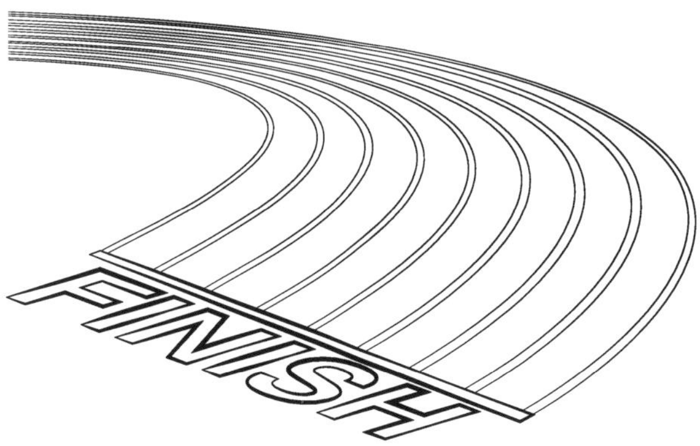

Task 5 **Do your dictation.**

Listen carefully and use the spelling, writing and punctuation that you have practised.

Name: ______________________________ Date: ______________

Task 1 **Reading practice**

Read the story.

A day at the beach

The three of us went to the beach in a jeep for a week's holiday. We took beef, beans, peas and ice-cream for each of us to eat. At the beach the heat from the sun was strong. We screamed with joy all the way to the sea. We swam in the deep sea and we also swam at the reef. But the reef was filled with seaweed so we spent most of our time on the beach.

Task 2 **Reading comprehension**

(a) Draw the story. (b) Label the *ea* and *ee* words.

Name: ______________________________ Date: ______________

Task 3 **Identify errors and correct them.**

(a) Find 15 spelling or punctuation errors and correct them.

A day at the beach

The threa of us whent to the beech in a jeep for a weak's holiday. We took beef, beens, peas and ice-cream for eech of us to eat. At the beach the heet from the sun was srong. We scream with joy all the wa to the sea. We swam in the deap sea and we also swam at the reaf. But the reaf was filled with seawead so we spent most of our time on the beech.

(b) Check your work. What was your score out of 15? ______

Task 4 **Copy the story carefully.**

Use your best pencil grip, writing posture and letter formations.

Task 5 **Do your dictation.**

Listen carefully and use the spelling, writing and punctuation that you have practised.

Name: ______________________________ Date: ______________

Task 1 **Reading practice**

Read the story.

Storm clouds

Over the house, clouds began to gather in the sky. Following this, the clouds darkened and a loud storm began to sound. Rain began to pound out from the clouds. The rain pounded over the ground. The rain pounded over the house and all around. The rain fell all around. An hour later, the clouds moved south and the sun came out once again.

Task 2 **Reading comprehension**

(a) Draw the story. (b) Label the *ou* words.

Name: ______________________________ Date: ______________

Task 3 **Identify errors and correct them.**

(a) Find 15 spelling or punctuation errors and correct them.

Storm clouds

Over the hous, clowds began to gather in the sky. following this, the clouds darkened and a lawd storm began to soond. Rain began to pound out from the clouds. The rane pounded ova the gound. The rain pounded over the house and all uround. The rain fel all around. An houa later, the cloads moved sowth and the sun came out wuns agen.

(b) Check your work. What was your score out of 15? ______

Task 4 **Copy the story carefully.**

Use your best pencil grip, writing posture and letter formations.

Task 5 **Do your dictation.**

Listen carefully and use the spelling, writing and punctuation that you have practised.

Name: ______________________ Date: ____________

Task 1 **Reading practice**

Read the story.

The mouse house

A mouse had a house underground. It was a sweet round underground house. The mouse was so proud of her house. The mouse liked to scout about on the ground for fresh nuts. Then the mouse would count out her nuts, put them in her pouch and run back into her house. The mouse would then sit on her couch and feast on her nuts.

Task 2 **Reading comprehension**

(a) Draw the story. (b) Label the *ou* words.

Name: ________________________________ Date: ______________

Task 3 **Identify errors and correct them.**

(a) Find 15 spelling or punctuation errors and correct them.

The mouse house

A mous had a hous undergrond. It was a sweet rond underground hose. The mouse was so prod of her house. The mouse liked to scout about on the grond for fresh nuts. Then the mous would cont out her nuts, poot them in her poch and run back into her hous. The mose would then sit on her coush and feast on her nut.

(b) Check your work. What was your score out of 15? ______

Task 4 **Copy the story carefully.**

Use your best pencil grip, writing posture and letter formations.

Task 5 **Do your dictation.**

Listen carefully and use the spelling, writing and punctuation that you have practised.

Name: ______________________ Date: ____________

Task 1 **Reading practice**

Read the story.

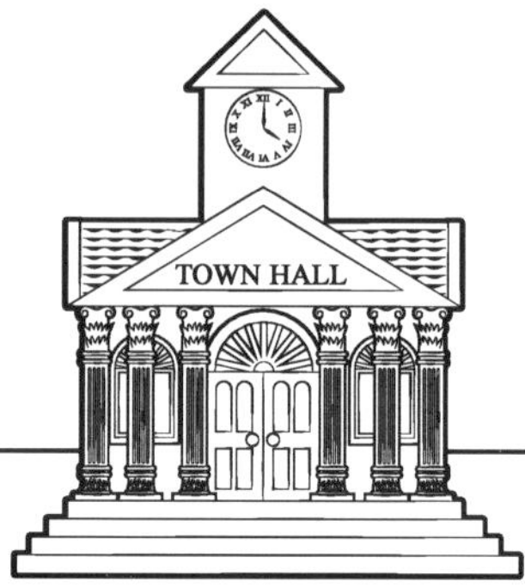

Power off in town

There was much happening in town. A crowd gathered down at the town hall. The crowd gathered to growl about how the town's power had been turned off. The crowd was ever so rowdy as they growled. Without power everyone was having cold showers. Next they stormed down to the power plant to try to sort out the town's power problem. The rowdy crowd was not keen on further cold showers.

Task 2 **Reading comprehension**

(a) Draw the story. (b) Label the *ow* words.

Name: ______________________________ Date: ______________

Task 3 **Identify errors and correct them.**

(a) Find 15 spelling or punctuation errors and correct them.

Power off in town

Where was much happening in town. A crowd gather down at the town holl. The crowd gather to growl about how the town's pouer had been turn off. The crowd wos ever so rowdy as thay growled. Without power everyone was haveing cold shower. Next they storm down to the power plant to try to sort owt the town's power probem. The rowdy crowd was not kean on further cold shower.

(b) Check your work. What was your score out of 15? ______

Task 4 **Copy the story carefully.**

Use your best pencil grip, writing posture and letter formations.

Task 5 **Do your dictation.**

Listen carefully and use the spelling, writing and punctuation that you have practised.

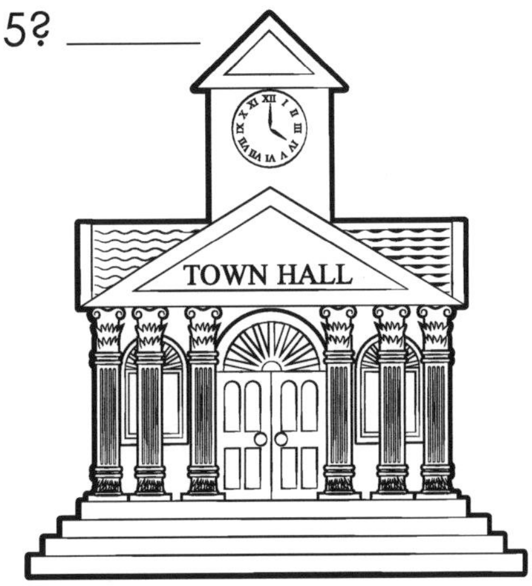

Name: ______________________ Date: ____________

Task 1 **Reading practice**

Read the story.

The brown clown

A clown had a frown. The clown was dressed in brown. The clown had brown jeans, a brown shirt, a brown crown and brown boots. The clown was in all brown and he felt down. He did think, 'I will not make the people in town happy. I will make them growl as I am all in brown'. So the frowning clown vowed to find red, green, blue and yellow to put on. The clown had a shower and put on a gold crown and a dress with flowers on it. The crowd will now be happy to see him.

Task 2 **Reading comprehension**

(a) Draw the story. (b) Label the ow words.

Name: ______________________ Date: ____________

Task 3 **Identify errors and correct them.**

(a) Find 15 spelling or punctuation errors and correct them.

The brown clown

A clown had a frown. The cloun was dress in brown. The clown had broun jeans, a broun shirt, a broun crown and brown boots. The clown was in all brown and he felt doun. He did think, 'I will not make the people in toun happy. I will make them groul as I am all in brown'. So the frouning clown vowed to find red, gren, blue and yellow to poot on. The cloun had a showu and put on a gold crown and a dress with flouers on it. The crowd will now be happe to see him.

(b) Check your work. What was your score out of 15? ______

Task 4 **Copy the story carefully.**

Use your best pencil grip, writing posture and letter formations.

Task 5 **Do your dictation.**

Listen carefully and use the spelling, writing and punctuation that you have practised.

Name: ______________________ Date: ____________

Task 1 **Reading practice**

Read the story.

An owl's nest

A brown owl did fly down from the clouds. Next the brown owl did fly around the town and then she did scout about for things for her nest. The owl went down to the ground for twigs. The owl also did scout about for bark and an amount of wood. Then the brown owl had no more scouting to do as the nest had been made.

Task 2 **Reading comprehension**

(a) Draw the story. (b) Label the *ou* and *ow* words.

Name: ______________________________ Date: ______________

Task 3 **Identify errors and correct them.**

(a) Find 15 spelling or punctuation errors and correct them.

An owl's nest

A broun owl did fly doun from the clowds. Next the brown oul did fly arownd the toun and then she did scowt abowt for things for her nest. The oul whent down to the grownd for twigs. The owl also did scout abowt for bark and an amownt of wood. Then the broun owl had no more scowting to do as the nest had been made.

(b) Check your work. What was your score out of 15? ______

Task 4 **Copy the story carefully.**

Use your best pencil grip, writing posture and letter formations.

Task 5 **Do your dictation.**

Listen carefully and use the spelling, writing and punctuation that you have practised.

Name: ______________________________ Date: ______________

Task 1 **Reading practice**

Read the story.

Drew's missing screws

Drew knew he needed to mend his bookshelf. Drew threw his new and his older books onto the carpet. Drew took a few moments to look at the bookshelf. Drew needed a few screws for the third shelf. Drew blew the dust from the third shelf and a few screws flew into the air. Drew then did screw in the few screws. Drew put the books back on the shelf and when he finished, Drew ate stew for his dinner.

Task 2 **Reading comprehension**

(a) Draw the story. (b) Label the *ew* words.

Name: ______________________________ Date: ____________

Task 3 **Identify errors and correct them.**

(a) Find 15 spelling or punctuation errors and correct them.

Drew's missing screws

Drew knoo he needed to mend his bookshelf. Drew throo his noo and his oldu books onto the carpet. Drew took a foo moment to look at the bookshelf. Drew needed a few scroos for the third shelf. Droo bloo the dust from the therd shelf and a foo screws floo into the air. Drew then did scroo in the few screws. Drew put the books back on the shelf and when he finish, Drew ate stoo for his dinner.

(b) Check your work. What was your score out of 15? ______

Task 4 **Copy the story carefully.**

Use your best pencil grip, writing posture and letter formations.

Task 5 **Do your dictation.**

Listen carefully and use the spelling, writing and punctuation that you have practised.

Name: ______________________________ Date: ______________

Task 1 **Reading practice**

Read the story.

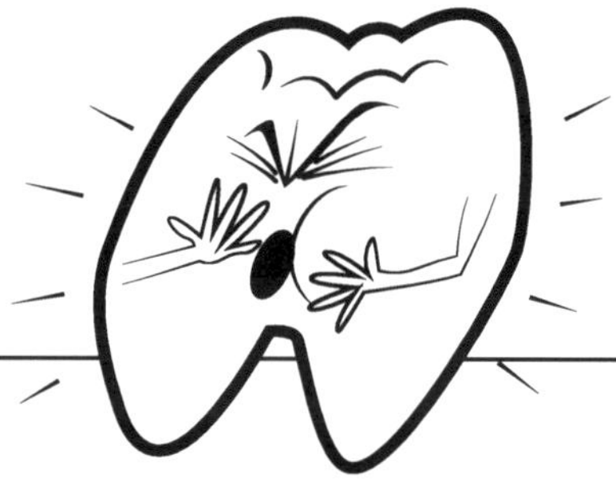

A tooth in pain

At noon a tooth started to chew on food. Then the tooth did chew on a few sweets. The tooth did chew on a few sweet plums and the tooth did even chew on a brew of stew. The tooth knew something bad had happened. A pain grew in the tooth. In a few moments the pain was so bad that the tooth had to tell his news to a dentist. He was lucky that the dentist knew what to do with the tooth.

Task 2 **Reading comprehension**

(a) Draw the story. (b) Label the *ew* and *oo* words.

Name: ______________________________ Date: ____________

Task 3 **Identify errors and correct them.**

(a) Find 15 spelling or punctuation errors and correct them.

A tooth in pain

At noon a toof started to choo on food. Then the tooth did choo on a foo sweets. The tooth did chew on a few sweat plums and the tooth did even chew on a brew of stoo. The tooth new somefing bad had happened. A pain groo in the tooth. In a few moment the pain was so bad that the toof had to tell his knews to a dentist. He was lucke that the dentis new what to do with the tooth.

(b) Check your work. What was your score out of 15? ______

Task 4 **Copy the story carefully.**

Use your best pencil grip, writing posture and letter formations.

Task 5 **Do your dictation.**

Listen carefully and use the spelling, writing and punctuation that you have practised.

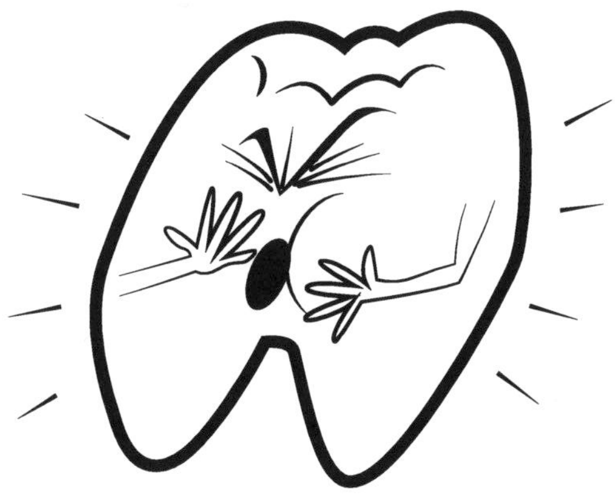

Name: ______________________ Date: ______________

Task 1 **Reading practice**

Read the story.

A rescue helped by a clue

Jim was good at sailing, but Jim did refuse to tell where he went. No-one had a clue where Jim sailed on the deep blue sea. Jim left only one clue. The clue was that he sailed true north. One day Jim did need a rescue and the clue helped the rescue party find him on the deep blue sea.

Task 2 **Reading comprehension**

(a) Draw the story. (b) Label the *ue* words.

Name: ______________________ Date: ____________

Task 3 **Identify errors and correct them.**

(a) Find 15 spelling or punctuation errors and correct them.

A rescue helped by a clue

Jim was good at sailing, but jim did refuse to tell where he whent. No-one had a cloo where Jim sailed on the deap blue see. Jim lefted onle one clue. The cloo was that he sailed true norf. One day jim did need a rescoo and the clue help the rescue parte find him on the deep bloo see.

(b) Check your work. What was your score out of 15? ______

Task 4 **Copy the story carefully.**

Use your best pencil grip, writing posture and letter formations.

Task 5 **Do your dictation.**

Listen carefully and use the spelling, writing and punctuation that you have practised.

Name: ______________________________ Date: ______________

Task 1 **Reading practice**

Read the story.

Is it true?

Is it true that owls do hoot at the zoo when the moon is up? Is it true that blue glue is stronger than white glue? Is it true that a dog can rescue a fox? Is it true that the moon has room for all of us to live on it? Is it true that noon is very soon and is it true that you can shoot a ball into a hoop? As I can give no clues, do think if each of these is true.

Task 2 **Reading comprehension**

(a) Draw the story. (b) Label the *ue* and *oo* words.

Name: ______________________ Date: ____________

Task 3 **Identify errors and correct them.**

(a) Find 15 spelling or punctuation errors and correct them.

Is it true?

Is it troo that owls do hoot at the zoo when the moon is up? Is it true that bloo glue is strongu than white gloo? Is it troo that a dog can rescoo a fox Is it true that the mon has rom for all of us to live on it? Is it true that noon is vere soon and is it true that you can shot a ball into a hoop? As I can give no cloos, doo thick if eech of these is true.

(b) Check your work. What was your score out of 15? ______

Task 4 **Copy the story carefully.**

Use your best pencil grip, writing posture and letter formations.

Task 5 **Do your dictation.**

Listen carefully and use the spelling, writing and punctuation that you have practised.

Name: ______________________ Date: ____________

Task 1 **Reading practice**

Read the story.

The puppy with no name

Today Mummy and Daddy got a puppy. Do we call the puppy Rocky, Dusty or Rusty? Do we call the puppy Sandy, Sunny or Windy? Still Mummy and Daddy have no name for the puppy. As the puppy with no name does make the house so messy, Mummy and Daddy think of the perfect name. We call the puppy Messy.

Task 2 **Reading comprehension**

(a) Draw the story. (b) Label the *y* words.

Name: ______________________ Date: __________

Task 3 **Identify errors and correct them.**

(a) Find 15 spelling or punctuation errors and correct them.

The puppy with no name

Today Mumme and Dadde got a puppe. Do we call the puppe Rocky, Duste or Ruste. Do we call the puppy Sandy, Sunny or Windy. Still Mumy and Dady have no name for the puppy. as the puppy with no name does make the howse so messe, Mummy and Daddy thick of the perfect name. We call the pupy Messy.

(b) Check your work. What was your score out of 15? ______

Task 4 **Copy the story carefully.**

Use your best pencil grip, writing posture and letter formations.

Task 5 **Do your dictation.**

Listen carefully and use the spelling, writing and punctuation that you have practised.

Name: ______________________ Date: ______________

Task 1 **Reading practice**

Read the story.

The puppy and the seeds

Mummy and Daddy had some seeds to plant. Mummy saw a sandy part of the garden beside the green trees and Daddy dug three deep holes for the seeds. It had been three weeks and the seeds had not peeped up. But Mummy and Daddy did not see the puppy dig up the seeds. I think the puppy did a funny thing.

Task 2 **Reading comprehension**

(a) Draw the story. (b) Label the *ee* and *y* words.

Name: ______________________ Date: ____________

Task 3 **Identify errors and correct them.**

(a) Find 15 spelling or punctuation errors and correct them.

The puppy and the seeds

Mumy and Daddy had some seeds to pant.

Mummy sore a sand part of the gardn beside the

green trees and Dady dug three deap holes for the

seads. It had been three weaks and the seads had

not peep up. But Mumy and Dadde did not

see the puppe dig up the seeds. I think the pupy

did a funny thing.

(b) Check your work. What was your score out of 15? ______

Task 4 **Copy the story carefully.**

Use your best pencil grip, writing posture and letter formations.

Task 5 **Do your dictation.**

Listen carefully and use the spelling, writing and punctuation that you have practised.

Name: ______________________ Date: ____________

Task 1 **Reading practice**

Read the story.

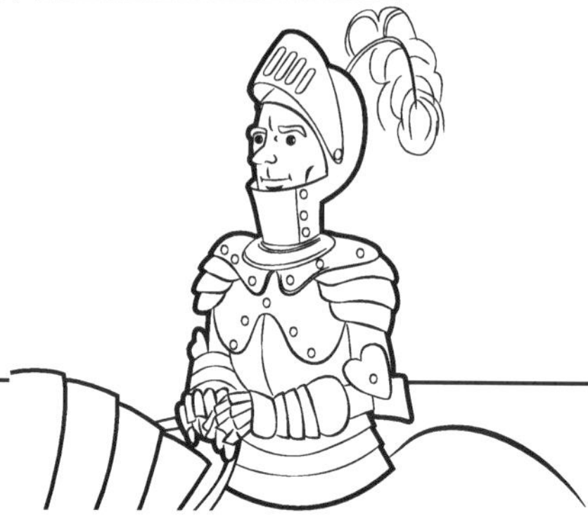

The knight's knife

The strong, brave knight knelt on one knee. As the strong, brave knight knelt on his knee he knocked a sharp knife. The sharp knife fell and cut a rope that had big knots in it. The knight needed to fix the rope with the knots in it. So the strong, clever knight found a knob of glue and fixed the rope with knots in it.

Task 2 **Reading comprehension**

(a) Draw the story. (b) Label the *kn* words.

Name: ______________________ Date: ____________

Task 3 **Identify errors and correct them.**

(a) Find 15 spelling or punctuation errors and correct them.

The knight's knife

The strong, brave night nelt on one nee. As the strong, brave night knelt on his nee he nocked a sharp nife. The sharp nife fell and cut a rope that had big nots in it. The night need to fix the rope with the nots in it. So the strong, clever night found a nob of glue and fixed the rope with nots in it.

(b) Check your work. What was your score out of 15? ______

Task 4 **Copy the story carefully.**

Use your best pencil grip, writing posture and letter formations.

Task 5 **Do your dictation.**

Listen carefully and use the spelling, writing and punctuation that you have practised.

Name: ______________________ Date: ____________

Task 1 **Reading practice**

Read the story.

The shy spy

The spy was sly, but she was also quite shy. The spy did try to be big and bold but she was still shy. One day the shy spy did look into a pig sty. The shy spy crept up on the pig sty and saw the pig fly out of the sty and into the sky. The spy then got an idea. If a pig can fly then maybe she can also fly. But the spy was shy and did not try to fly.

Task 2 **Reading comprehension**

(a) Draw the story. (b) Label the *y* words.

Name: ____________________ Date: ____________

Task 3 **Identify errors and correct them.**

(a) Find 15 spelling or punctuation errors and correct them.

The shy spy

The spi was sly, but she was also kwite shi. The spy did tri to be big and bold but she was still shi. One day the shy spy did look to a pig sti. The shy spy krept up on the pig sty and seed the pig fly owt of the sty and into the ski. The spy then got a idea. If a pig can fly then maybe she can also fli. But the spy wos shy and did not tri to fly.

(b) Check your work. What was your score out of 15? ______

Task 4 **Copy the story carefully.**

Use your best pencil grip, writing posture and letter formations.

Task 5 **Do your dictation.**

Listen carefully and use the spelling, writing and punctuation that you have practised.

Appendix

Contents

Templates for:

- Copying and writing (Task 4)
- Dictation (Task 5)
- Writing line formats for 5- to 7- and 8- to 9-year-olds

Name: ______________________ Date: ____________

Task 4 Copying and writing

With your best writing posture, pencil grip and letter formation, rewrite the story from Task 1.

Title of the story:

Stop! Think! Before I finish, have I read over and checked my work? ☐ Yes ☐ No

Stop! Think! Before I finish, have I read over and checked my work? ☐ Yes ☐ No

Name: ______________________________ Date: ______________

Task 5 Dictation

The story will be read (i.e. dictated) and you will need to write the story. You will need to listen carefully. You will also need to use the spelling, writing and punctuation that have been practised in previous tasks.

(Adult to discuss with child and choose only one goal from those listed below.) **Today, I am trying to:**				✓ Choose one.
Writing goals	☐ remember the size of my letters and their placement on the dark lines	A listening goal	☐ listen carefully.	**Dictation attempt:**
	☐ remember not to mix up my upper-case and lower-case letters	Spelling goals	☐ sound out as I spell words ☐ correctly use my phonic skills.	1. ☐ 2. ☐ 3. ☐
	☐ use a proper pencil grip and sit with correct posture.	A punctuation goal	☐ remember capital letters and full stops.	
A personal goal:				

Title of the story: ______________________________

Stop! Think! Before I finish, have I read over and checked my work? ☐ Yes ☐ No

Stop! Think! Before I finish, have I read over and checked my work? ☐ Yes ☐ No

Name: ____________________ Date: __________

Task 4 Copying and writing

With your best writing posture, pencil grip and letter formation, rewrite the story from Task 1.

Title of the story: ____________________

Stop! Think! Before I finish, have I read over and checked my work? ☐ Yes ☐ No

Stop! Think! Before I finish, have I read over and checked my work? ☐ Yes ☐ No

Name: ______________________ Date: ____________

Task 5 Dictation

The story will be read (i.e. dictated) and you will need to write the story. You will need to listen carefully. You will also need to use the spelling, writing and punctuation that have been practised in previous tasks.

(Adult to discuss with child and choose only one goal from those listed below.) **Today, I am trying to:**				✓ Choose one. **Dictation attempt:**
Writing goals	☐ remember the size of my letters and their placement on the dark lines	A listening goal	☐ listen carefully.	1. ☐
	☐ remember not to mix up my upper-case and lower-case letters	Spelling goals	☐ sound out as I spell words ☐ correctly use my phonic skills.	2. ☐
	☐ use a proper pencil grip and sit with correct posture.	A punctuation goal	☐ remember capital letters and full stops.	3. ☐
A personal goal:				

Title of the story: ______________________

Stop! Think! Before I finish, have I read over and checked my work? ☐ Yes ☐ No

Stop! Think! Before I finish, have I read over and checked my work? ☐ Yes ☐ No

Name: ______________________ Date: ____________

Task 4 Copying and writing

With your best writing posture, pencil grip and letter formation, rewrite the story from Task 1.

Title of the story:

Stop! Think! Before I finish, have I read over and checked my work? ☐ Yes ☐ No

Stop! Think! Before I finish, have I read over and checked my work? ☐ Yes ☐ No

Name: ______________________ Date: ____________

Task 5 Dictation

The story will be read (i.e. dictated) and you will need to write the story. You will need to listen carefully. You will also need to use the spelling, writing and punctuation that have been practised in previous tasks.

(Adult to discuss with child and choose only one goal from those listed below.) **Today, I am trying to:**				✓ Choose one.
Writing goals	☐ remember the size of my letters and their placement on the dark lines	A listening goal	☐ listen carefully.	**Dictation attempt:**
	☐ remember not to mix up my upper-case and lower-case letters	Spelling goals	☐ sound out as I spell words ☐ correctly use my phonic skills.	1. ☐ 2. ☐ 3. ☐
	☐ use a proper pencil grip and sit with correct posture.	A punctuation goal	☐ remember capital letters and full stops.	
A personal goal:				

Title of the story: ______________________

Stop! Think! Before I finish, have I read over and checked my work? ☐ Yes ☐ No

Stop! Think! Before I finish, have I read over and checked my work? ☐ Yes ☐ No